T0153339

Prayer

&

Meditation

AA members share the many ways
they connect spiritually

AAGRAPEVINE,Inc.

New York, New York
WWW. AAGRAPEVINE.ORG

BOOKS PUBLISHED BY AA GRAPEVINE, INC.

The Language of the Heart (& eBook)
The Best of the Grapevine Volumes I, II, III
The Best of Bill (& eBook)
Thank You for Sharing
Spiritual Awakenings (& eBook)
I Am Responsible: The Hand of AA
The Home Group: Heartbeat of AA (& eBook)
Emotional Sobriety—The Next Frontier (& eBook)
Spiritual Awakenings II (& eBook)
In Our Own Words: Stories of Young AAs in Recovery (& eBook)
Beginners' Book (& eBook)
Voices of Long-Term Sobriety (& eBook)
A Rabbit Walks Into A Bar
Step by Step—Real AAs, Real Recovery (& eBook)
Emotional Sobriety II—The Next Frontier (& eBook)
Young & Sober (& eBook)
Into Action (& eBook)
Happy, Joyous & Free (& eBook)
One on One (& eBook)
No Matter What (& eBook)
Grapevine Daily Quote Book (& eBook)
Sober & Out (& eBook)
Forming True Partnerships (& eBook)
Our Twelve Traditions (& eBook)
Making Amends (& eBook)
Voices of Women in AA (& eBook)
AA in the Military (& eBook)
One Big Tent (& eBook)
Take Me to Your Sponsor (& eBook)
Free on the Inside (& eBook)

IN SPANISH

El lenguaje del corazón
Lo mejor de Bill (& eBook)
El grupo base: Corazón de AA
Lo mejor de La Viña
Felices, alegres y libres (& eBook)
Un día a la vez (& eBook)
Frente A Frente (& eBook)
Bajo El Mismo Techo (& eBook)

IN FRENCH

Le langage du coeur
Les meilleurs articles de Bill
Le Groupe d'attache: Le battement du coeur des AA
En tête à tête (& eBook)
Heureux, joyeux et libres (& eBook)
La sobriété émotive

Prayer
&
Meditation

AA members share the many ways
they connect spiritually

AAGRAPEVINE,Inc.

New York, New York

WWW. AAGRAPEVINE.ORG

AA Preamble

Alcoholics Anonymous is a fellowship of people
who share their experience, strength and hope with each
other that they may solve their common problem
and help others to recover from alcoholism.

The only requirement for membership is a desire to stop drinking.
There are no dues or fees for AA membership;
we are self-supporting through our own contributions.
AA is not allied with any sect, denomination, politics, organization
or institution; does not wish to engage in any controversy,
neither endorses nor opposes any causes.

Our primary purpose is to stay sober
and help other alcoholics to achieve sobriety.

©*AA Grapevine, Inc.*

Contents

AA Preamble . . . . *V*
Welcome . . . . *XI*

PART I

A Journey Into Prayer & Meditation

CHAPTER ONE
Daily Routines
Members fold prayer and meditation into their sober lives

Meditation Made Easy *April 2009* *4*
The Tedium and Terror *November 2012* *5*
To Improve Our Conscious Contact With God
  November 2005 . . . . *7*
Holy Order of Doorknobs *September 2012* *7*
A Daily Meditation *September 2011* *9*
Who's Under the Hood? *April 1986* *13*
Tuning In to Our Higher Power *November 1993* *15*

CHAPTER TWO

Well-Worn Paths

Many AAs look to traditional religions and practices

A Deeper Look *November 2017* 18

Prayer *January 1980* 22

Into the Woods *September 2007* 23

Finds Lord's Prayer Key to Steps *September 1946* 25

As the Spirit Moves Us *February 2021* 27

Many Steps to Prayer *November 2018* 32

Stronger & Brighter *November 2015* 35

I Don't Need to Understand *November 2020* 37

The Answer to My Prayer *September 2019* 39

CHAPTER THREE

Getting There Through Action

Practicing a spiritual connection while running, exercising, swimming and more

Calm and Quiet *November 2019* 44

To Sink...Or Swim? *July 1954* 46

Back in the Saddle Again *February 1989* 49

Trudging the Road of Happy Destiny *December 2011* 51

A Serene Place at 5:00 A.M. *September 1980* 53

Sink or Swim *December 2016* 54

Two Wheel Contact *November 2012* 57

Sk8ting Through Life *September 2005* 58

CHAPTER FOUR

The Serenity Prayer

Using a beloved prayer to connect and pray

These Twenty-Five Words *April 1979* 64

Hula Hoop Larry and the Serenity Prayer *January 2020* 65

Attitude Adjustment *November 1997* 67

Sounds of Silence *April 2004*. *69*
Dear HP *November 2014* *71*
An Answer Without a Prayer *April 1986*. *73*
OK With Me *August 2006*. *75*

CHAPTER FIVE

Stars, Mountains, Water and Furry Creatures
Finding a spiritual connection through nature and the universe

A Thousand Wishes *March 2015* *80*
Rock Bottom *July 2009*. *82*
Under the Ginkgo Tree *February 2011* *84*
Higher Power Unleashed *November 2016* *85*
Under the Stars *November 2016* *87*
Time to Pray *April 2021*. *88*
A Walk in the Park *August 2008*. *91*
A Fox in the Woods *October 2001*. *92*
Wonderfully Humbling *April 2018* *94*
Perfect Timing *May 2015* *97*

PART II

Techniques & Practices
There are many ways to pray and meditate

The Highest Form of Prayer *January 1987*. *100*
Lost—and Found—at Sea *December 1987* *101*
A Sacred Safari *April 2004*. *103*
Conscious Contact *November 1991* *105*
Binge Thinker *July 2010*. *106*
Staying in the Day *April 2021* *107*
Believing *January 1980* *109*

Alcoholic's Meditation *November 2010* *110*

Many Powers Greater Than Me *February 2019* *111*

Sitting in Silence, Listening *November 2009* *113*

First Things First *November 1991* *114*

Divine Hot Line *December 1977* *116*

Spending Time With God *November 2016.* *120*

Twelve Steps *122*

Twelve Traditions *123*

About AA and AA Grapevine *124*

Welcome

Alcoholism is often referred to as a threefold illness: physical, mental and spiritual. And Alcoholics Anonymous has always offered, since its very inception, a pathway to recovery on all three levels.

In this book, AA members describe the many different aspects of the spiritual connection that animates their recovery. From discovering spirituality in their daily lives to practicing prayer and meditation on a regular basis, these alcoholics have found how important a spiritual connection is to gaining and maintaining sobriety. The following pages contain chapters on daily routines, traditional religious practices, activities and exercise, techniques, nature and the Serenity Prayer. This is not a "how to" book, rather it's an inspiring collection of shared experiences by alcoholics who have put down the drink and are trying to expand their spiritual connection in recovery through prayer and meditation.

Humanity has historically turned to religion and the many manifestations of spirituality to help explain life's countless mysteries—and alcoholics are no exception in the age-old search for answers. In fact, the roots of spiritual experience stretch far back into AA's history, back even further than our cofounders Bill W. and Dr. Bob's first meeting in Akron. In the early 1920s, Dr. Carl Jung, the noted Swiss psychiatrist, treated a hopeless alcoholic named Rowland H., with whom he was making little headway. Jung noted, however, that Rowland might find some hope for recovery if he could, as Bill W. later related, "become the subject of a spiritual or religious experience—in short, a genuine conversion." Rowland did eventually find a conversion experience and became connected with the Oxford Groups in New York City, where he helped a fellow named Ebby T. get sober.

Ebby, an old friend, ultimately carried the message of recovery to Bill W. who, in New York City's Towns Hospital, had a spiritual experience of his own which propelled him into sobriety.

An integral part of the AA program from its earliest days, this formula of using spirituality to combat alcoholism has provided AA members with a pathway to gaining and maintaining recovery. The stories in this book clearly show how AA members of all descriptions continue making new and relevant the ancient practices of prayer and meditation. Who knew that spirituality could be found on a bicycle heading downhill at breakneck speed...in a swimming pool...or in a confrontation with a rattlesnake?

As Emily G. writes in "Spending Time With God," the book's final story, "I truly believed that other AA members had access to some sort of secret prayer and meditation manual that instructed them how to properly pray, meditate, talk to and hear direction straight from God." Well, of course Emily found that there *is* no secret manual. But the stories in this book do highlight the important role that prayer and meditation play in AA members' lives, as well as illustrate many ways to get there. And "the best part," Emily writes, "is that there is no wrong way to do it."

PART I

*A Journey Into Prayer
& Meditation*

CHAPTER ONE

Daily Routines

Members fold prayer and meditation into their sober lives

In AA we hear that the only thing a person needs to get started with prayer and meditation is an open mind. But just how does one acquire this precious attribute? According to the anonymous author of this chapter's opening story, "Meditation Made Easy," it can be as simple as asking for help. Noting, "I had absolutely no idea how to pray or meditate," this writer pressed ahead, "swallowing my pride as only the desperate can," and asked for some guidance. Over time, this member settled into a routine of just "talking to God," and before long, "I gave him an earful."

For many, like Gary T. in his letter "To Improve Our Conscious Contact With God," maintaining and developing a conscious contact with a Higher Power can be as simple and as deeply profound as developing a relationship with another person. "I can talk. I can be silent. I can ask favors. I can forgive," he writes. But others, like J.H. in the article "Holy Order of Doorknobs," have had a tougher time with the Higher Power concept. "My experiences with organized religion left me quite confused, angry and belligerent," J.H. writes, yet "alcohol had me beat." And having heard at a meeting that "my Higher Power could be anything I wanted it to be—even a doorknob!" this writer thought it was time to give it a shot.

However, when a person chooses to "tune in" to God's will—and the ways are many—the results can provide added protection against a drink. As George B. in his story "Tuning In to our Higher Power" notes, "The first step in seeking God's will is that of becoming receptive to it!"

Meditation Made Easy
April 2009

At a counseling session not long after my first AA meeting, my counselor urged me to pray and meditate. Normally, I would have quietly refused, while offering some frivolous excuse such as not having the time. Somehow though, the freedom that AA was giving me to decide such matters for myself enabled me to acquire an open mind on the subject of spirituality for the first time in my life. The only problem was that I had absolutely no idea how to pray or meditate. Swallowing my pride as only the desperate can, I asked the counselor for help.

She said I should pray to whatever I thought might be out there. I was advised to ask this something to keep me sober for just this day and, if I hadn't taken a drink by the end of the day, I should offer my thanks to the same whatever it was. That sounded almost too simple. Of course I would try prayer. What did I have to lose? To this day I say those same prayers every morning and night and I, who could never stay away from a drink longer than two days, have gone a decade and a half without a desire for one.

Meditation hasn't been so easy. Strangely, the people at that one meeting I attended were no help. I heard some say to sit quietly and empty my mind. Others said to recite some passage from the Big Book or other spiritual text over and over. Some merely shrugged and said prayer was enough, as long as I was sincere. Then there were those inclined toward nature, who advocated walks in the woods or watching the sun set. I leaned toward this approach, but soon found my mind wandering. My counselor recommended talking to God. This was a little tricky, since I was still dabbling in agnosticism. However, I had agreed to go to any length and to keep an open mind.

For my job I had to face a half hour drive each way. "Talking to God" seemed farfetched but, as it turned out, I gave him an earful to and from my new place of employment.

Even after changing jobs, my talks with God on the way to and from work became routine. They began to take the form of a real conversation rather than simply venting steam. In time, I acquired the ability to begin talking with no thought of what was going to come out of my mouth. During these "conversations" the car radio stayed off. I found that the world's problems would still be there whether I listened to the news or not. Interestingly, those worldly problems had less impact on me after God and I had discussed the more immediate issues swirling around inside my head. I began to look forward to these times set apart with God. The difference between meditation and prayer became apparent. Meditation, practiced in the form of simply talking to whatever I thought might be there, was helping to change my life. I could deal with life now rather than running to a bottle and momentary oblivion. I quit the debating society over whether God is or isn't. I made my decision that God is. AA led me to him and meditation was the principal means by which we communicated. I could never have imagined that meditation, which has played such a vital role in my recovery, could be as simple as having a conversation.

Anonymous

The Tedium and Terror
November 2012

A section from "A Vision For You" from our Big Book is often read at the end of our AA meeting. The words "abandon yourself to God" resonated for me today, and I pondered their meaning. As I learned early in my AA journey, a place to start is with a dictionary.

Abandon: "to give up with the intent of never again claiming a right or interest in." How do I do this? How do I give up myself with the intent of never again claiming a right or interest in? The Third and Eleventh Steps are my guideposts. In the Third Step, I begin the practice of offering myself to God to take me and to do what God wants with me. Fortunately, the Third Step Prayer also includes the removal of my difficulties. That's the part of the prayer I like best because, in the face of problems, my default position is to run and hide, to take off in a full flight from reality. To pray for the removal of my difficulties gives me comfort that I can stay where I am and wait for the difficulties to be removed.

The Eleventh Step provides straightforward directions on how to abandon myself to God. All I need to do is pray for knowledge of God's will for me and the power to carry that out. Simple, right? It's easy to practice the Eleventh Step when I'm on day four of a two-week vacation in Hawaii walking along the beach. The decisions of the day are reduced to where to have breakfast and when to take a nap. OK God, got it, I'll let you decide.

But on a typical Monday morning as I contemplate a week of work, I am not inclined to pray simply. Then my anxious thoughts fill me with dread and my serenity is gone. My prayers become more like those of the wanderer in the desert looking for water. I implore God to let me win the lottery and be relieved of the tedium and terror of work. So far, those prayers for immediate wealth have not been answered.

When I can remember my days of early sobriety, I am reminded of how the grace of God saved me. At that time, my little world was falling apart and I was consumed with fear. I asked God for help and found myself in a meeting of AA. It was there I discovered that I had a loving God in my life. It was there I discovered I was not alone. It was there I discovered the tools that led to a spiritual awakening.

Through the work of the Twelve Steps, I can now relax and take it easy and know that, just for today, I don't have to worry. God is with me and will show me the way.

Michele C.
Davis, California

To Improve Our Conscious Contact With God
From: Dear Grapevine
November 2005

Maintaining and developing a conscious contact with my Higher Power, whom I choose to call God, can be as simple, and as deeply profound, as developing a relationship with another person. I can talk. I can be silent. I can ask favors. I can forgive. I believe that every encounter I have with another person is potentially an opportunity for prayer and meditation, for acknowledging and recognizing my Higher Power's presence within me and around me. And the more I seek the love and beauty of God's grace in the people around me, the more aware I become of God's presence in the world.

Gary T.
Poughkeepsie, New York

Holy Order of Doorknobs
September 2012

When I was a newcomer to Alcoholics Anonymous, I had a tough time with the Higher Power concept. My experiences with organized religion left me quite confused, angry and belligerent. I heard at a meeting that my Higher Power could be anything I wanted it to be—even a doorknob! My sponsor agreed.

A doorknob? "The Lord is my Doorknob, I shall not...lock?" This floored me. It was so weird, but I was intrigued. I had not heard of any "Holy Order of Doorknobs," and if I had to find a Higher Power of some kind to stay sober, would this work?

I was willing. Alcohol had me beat. I knew that. So starting Steps Two and Three, I went home that night and really thought about making my Higher Power a doorknob. I'd been agnostic up to that point, so I figured it wasn't that much of a stretch to make a Higher Power out of some sort of random piece of hardware.

That night, before I went to bed, I drew the curtains, made sure no one was around (I lived alone, but I had to be sure), got on my knees and said half-jokingly: "Oh Holy Doorknob, thank you for another day alive and sober, I pray for the alcoholic who still suffers, I ask for a good night's sleep and we'll see ya tomorrow."

And I went to bed. I slept well!

The next day, I woke up and headed to the bathroom where I encountered my first visit with my new Higher Power. The bathroom door was closed. What was weird was that I actually remembered my prayer from the night before! I knew that I would either need to open the door or explore other options, none of which were easier or softer (or sanitary)!

So I acknowledged my Higher Power Doorknob and opened the door. Once there, I saw the toilet lid down. I looked at that as kind of a door also. The shower also had a glass door on it. All of the knobs and handles on the kitchen cabinets and faucets got me through my coffee and breakfast before I even considered leaving the apartment—through another door.

As I prepared for work and locked the door to my apartment (another doorknob!) I got into my car (door handle) drove to my work as a ...housekeeper in a hotel! Every day at work I knocked on 12 doors, which I had to open to do my job, and of course, each room had a doorknob (on both sides of the door, by the way). On this particular day someone was out sick so I had an additional five more rooms to clean than normal. Throughout the day I acknowledged each doorknob silently to myself. It was a consistent and constant reminder.

After work I went to the local supermarket. As I stood outside the sliding doors it occurred to me that here there was no doorknob, so as far as this was concerned, there was no Higher Power here. Unless the floor mat that opens the door...

As I stood there staring at the floor mat in front of the grocery store wondering whether God existed or not, a lady came out with her grocery cart and said hello. I said hello and immediately walked in. Ha! I thought. Didn't need God for that door. But then another thought crossed my mind: What if God had sent that lady to open the door for me so I could go inside? Was I sure that wasn't the case? Could God send helpers? I didn't know. Why not?

I decided right then to surrender. God either is or he isn't. What is our choice to be? It didn't matter whether you believed in my doorknob or not. My life is easier if I use doorknobs. Otherwise I'm trapped behind walls, just like drinking again.

The day before my prayer, I had used doorknobs without a thought or care and they still worked. I had been using my Higher Power throughout my life, but had never realized it. I never made the connection. Once I realized that a Higher Power was indeed working in my life I started to try to reconnect back to that power to complete the circuit. That's when the magic started happening, the fourth dimension spoken of in the Big Book, when life suddenly becomes open and exciting! The rest of the Steps helped me find my way and clear the wreckage of my past.

So the doorknob has become a powerful symbol for me in my recovery. I was trapped when I was out there drinking. A power greater than myself for me turned out to be a doorknob. It set me free. And it wasn't even locked.

J.H.
Redondo Beach, California

A Daily Meditation
Online Exclusive
September 2011

I got up this morning, and rolled off the bed to my knees to get the day off the ground right like it says to do on pages 86 and 87 of the Big Book. I felt disorganized and disgruntled. I knew from past experience that if I let this thinking continue that it was going to screw up my day. It is always best for me to get my head right by following these directions. I am not sure of all the day has in store for me, other than plans that I made yesterday. But at least I am making a good attempt for positive outcomes for my endeavors.

The result is always up to God. It is amazing to me how I like to think that I am OK without asking God to empower me for the day ahead. I had to go through quite a long period in my own personal desert before I could convince myself that not only am I powerless over alcohol and drugs, people, places and things, but also myself.

I have found that if I do not get God into my life upon awakening, then I am self-will run riot. I want God's power in my life today, for there is a lot to do. I am tired of my insisting that I can do it myself without God's help, as though I were a 4-year-old in rebellion against my parents.

I grew tired of rebelling a long time ago, and in this sweet state of surrender, I was able to let go of that old idea that I can sustain myself on my own steam. I have those two pages memorized and I allow myself to take my time going through them. I like to be thorough with them. These are the instructions on how to not only stay sober for the day, but also to keep the consciousness of God in my mind. The longer I stay sober, the more I am aware of how much I need this God consciousness.

I drank my morning coffee down quickly this morning. I had only a little while before I had to go to a cleaning job. And I had to get it done by nine o'clock. So I sat there and gave myself a few moments to think as I drank my coffee. I thought about the presence of God. I was thinking about how when I practice this belief, whatever I am doing gets done a lot more quickly and efficiently than when I am lost in my own little world. I told myself as I sat that I was going to be aware of that presence for as much time as possible while I was doing my job because I wanted it to get done quickly and correctly.

It is easy for me to practice this Presence while I am here in my spot at home. For me, it is a meditation. I am still in the near silence of the house in the early morning. But when I am doing it "on the go," I am moving about and doing things. I have to consciously hold my mind in focus on this idea and be aware of my breathing. For some reason this helps.

When I first started to do this practice, it was not easy at all. I was in such a bad habit of attaching myself to the first ugly thought that my mind conjured up and running with it like I was a string tied around a boulder bouncing down a mountain in an avalanche. Before I knew it, the day was in shambles because of errors that I made.

It was hard for me to make the connection that my thinking had anything to do with the way my day went. Though the physical evidence can be overwhelming, I am one to want to rationalize away results and responsibility. It was tough for me to see that I am the cause of my own problems, just like it says in the book.

I made this connection between God consciousness and how my day went by going to meetings and listening to others, plus concentrated efforts on working the Steps—Steps Six and Seven in particular. My character defects can be like wild dogs. If they are not leashed first thing in the morning, they are not likely to be caught until later on in that day when I will finally pause and think, What am I doing? God, help me! So I take this time in the morning seriously and I find that I have a good habit for a change.

When I am still and focusing on my breathing, this brings on a very strong feeling of what I call a meditative state. I breathe in slowly and deeply, allowing my belly to expand before my chest does. I hold it in for a few seconds and then I exhale just as slowly, releasing the air from my chest and then my belly.

I think about God being present with me, all around me and through me with every breath I take. And then I get this wonderful feeling. My whole body is very heavy with relaxation. My forehead, in the center of it, feels different from the rest of my head. It is like there is something there, something heavy within it. It doesn't hurt or anything; just a spot right there smack in the center of my forehead, feels like the size of a quarter; a spot of something and it feels wonderful.

I don't know what it is but I love that sensation. When I have it, all the cares and concerns and worries that would be going on remain silent, somewhere in the depths of my lower consciousness. My character defects, the wild dogs, are asleep for the moment. For the truth is in that moment, they are not realities. They are past tense things that I thought about habitually in order to bring on those familiar sensations of fear and frustration and powerlessness that I was so used to feeling before I began to choose this practice.

But now that I am into the sensation of peace, I am a lot less inclined to choose to think on them first thing. And I am very aware of the discomfort I am feeling when I realize I am thinking about them. I go to work and my mind does its best to wander away from my chosen thoughts of God. I am aware of this and I change my focus. While I am moving about doing things, I do not yet get that totally relaxed feeling, but for whatever reason, the work gets done right in a lot less time than it would take if I thought about the usual stuff I think about when I am not spiritually focused.

I am aware of myself doing things, thinking stuff like, God works through me, and it gets done. Tasks are completed and I look up at the clock and the hands will have moved only a little. But if I had thought about my cares and worries, it would have taken me a lot longer to get it all done.

After the job is finished, I thank God for empowering me so that I could get the job done so well. The majority of the day still lies ahead of me, so I thank God for continuing to be with me as we go from moment to moment; activity to activity. I am peaceful in my head even though there is a lot on tap for the day. But I know that so long as I maintain this consciousness of God in mind, I will be able to deal with whatever happens.

I am so grateful for this way of life given to me freely by Alcoholics Anonymous. I am grateful that I am an alcoholic in this program, for I have never heard of being able to get all of this anywhere else.

Judy M.
Bluffton, South Carolina

Who's Under the Hood?
April 1986

I was nearly struck drunk the other day. Well, not really. I know there's no such thing. But I found out what that phrase can mean.

I had managed to get through (somehow) nearly two years of sobriety without experiencing a compulsion to drink. I continued going to six or seven AA meetings per week because I feared, in the back of my mind, that if I ever did have that compulsion I would yield to it. I am totally without willpower and believe firmly in immediate gratification.

The other day was a Monday. Mondays can be rough in my job, and maybe this one was a little rougher than usual. As I crossed the parking lot at 5:00 P.M. I felt worn out emotionally and physically. The idea of taking a drink never entered my mind. But suddenly, there it was: the urge to drink.

All at once, it seemed like the most natural thing to do was to stop somewhere on the way home, pick up a bottle of "sippin' whiskey," then sit down and relax—for three or four days!

Now, I had often thought about drinking. That was all right. When I thought about it, it did not seem like a real smart idea. Thinking, I could handle. ("Think before you drink," etc.) But this was not a thought or an idea. This was what they call a genuine compulsion.

I knew right away I could not handle it. However, I did remember that I had choices. At that moment these choices could be listed as follows: 1) Get drunk. 2) Go to a meeting. 3) Call my sponsor. 4) Pray.

I knew I couldn't exercise choices 2 or 3 in the middle of a parking lot. The earliest AA meeting I knew of didn't start for an hour and a half, and my sponsor might not be home for hours. And I might not last that long! (Immediate gratification, remember?) That left only 1 and 4. However, prayer is not something that comes naturally to me. "Sought through prayer and meditation." Meditation was fine. Meditation can be scientifically verified; you put people in a quiet room, hook them up to a brainwave machine and have them meditate. You know meditation works because you can watch the alpha waves. But prayer was another matter. I had never quite accepted the idea that there might be a Higher Power that was interested in me personally.

Then again, there was nothing to lose. I reflected in the parking lot that if it didn't work, I could still get drunk. So I said a very short prayer. Something like: "OK, Higher Power. If you really exist, please remove this burden. Period."

I mentioned before that I insist on immediate gratification. Naturally this principle includes prayer.

Almost as I reached my car, I heard my name being called from across the lot. I turned to see someone running toward me and waving. It was a man I knew slightly in the office and whose name I could not at the moment remember. I waited, wondering what he could possibly want.

"Do you have a pair of jumper cables?" he asked.

"No," I answered. Then I asked astutely, "What's the matter? Your car won't start?" He affirmed this was the case. "Dead battery?" I asked.

"No, the battery's OK." (At this point I began to suspect he knew less about cars than I do.) We walked back to his vehicle, discussing the problem.

"Maybe we could push-start it," I suggested. This sounded like a good idea until I learned his car had an automatic transmission. "Maybe the carburetor's flooded," I suggested. "Do you have a carburetor or fuel injectors?" He didn't know.

We went on for several minutes like this, taking inventory of my friend's car. Finally he decided to try starting it again. He got behind the wheel and turned the switch. The engine started at once, purring like a kitten. After that, my friend could only shrug, grin, thank me and drive off.

"Any time," I told him.

Then I walked back toward my own car, ready for my mind to take up its previous train of misery. Except I found that I didn't have to. For some reason my previous compulsion was gone.

As I drove home without stopping, I wondered about what had just happened. I remembered the brief prayer I had uttered before this incident. I remembered also my unspoken demand of God for immediate gratification. At first I couldn't see the connection. But then again, my "need" for a drink was gone.

After all, the message wasn't hard to figure out. My Higher Power was trying to tell me something like this: "As long as you are doing something for someone else—even if he only thinks he needs your help—you will be OK." In this case, immediate gratification was followed by immediate gratitude.

B. B.
San Francisco, California

Tuning In to Our Higher Power
November 1993

I had heard the last half of the Eleventh Step many times in meetings: "...praying only for knowledge of His will for us and the power to carry that out," yet I often wondered just how one can learn about God's will.

One day during an Eleventh Step meeting someone spoke of "tuning in" to God's will through regular periods of prayer and meditation. A picture of the TV set at home flashed across my mind. I saw myself twisting the knob to change channels, and with this came a new approach (for me) to this part of the Eleventh Step.

When I want to pick up the picture from a television station, I don't start by asking the station engineer to tune the signal to the place on the dial where my TV is set. Instead, I turn the knob at home to find the channel that carries that broadcast signal. In other words, I adjust to the station's setting instead of expecting it to comply with mine.

Might not the same thing be true for the signals that come from my Higher Power?

Viewed this way the entire purpose of prayer and meditation becomes that of focusing on God's will for me instead of asking for this or that according to my will at the moment. Instead of expecting my Higher Power to change things to suit me (the equivalent of asking a TV station to move its signal to the channel where my dial is set), I need to focus my daily period of quiet meditation on creating a condition within myself that opens me up to, and accepts, God's will for me. The first step in seeking God's will is that of becoming receptive to it!

Since that day when the image of the TV set came to mind I've felt so much more in tune with the entire purpose of the Eleventh Step. The act of focusing on God's will—as we are told to do in the second part of the Step—increases my success with the first portion that deals with improving my conscious contact with God as I understand him.

The "Twelve and Twelve" tells us that when we catch a glimpse of God's will for us, and focus on the real and eternal things of life such as love and truth, we are no longer deeply disturbed by many smaller things that surround us in our daily affairs. Tuning in to a Higher Power truly leads to greater serenity—and to a much richer way of life!

George B.
Alexandria, Virginia

CHAPTER TWO

Well-Worn Paths

Many AAs look to traditional religions and practices

I n AA there is no "one size fits all" conception of a Higher Power and each AA is free to fashion whatever works given a person's own experience. For some that experience includes traditional religion or the return to a practice that might have been abandoned in the madcap pursuit of alcohol. Logically woven together, as Mike S. notes in the chapter's opening story, "A Deeper Look," the result can be deeply rewarding: "The practice of my religion strengthens my AA program, while my experience of powerlessness and humility and amends and forgiveness in AA infuses a deep personal meaning into my religion. They work hand in hand."

Bill C. in his story "Finds Lord's Prayer Key to Steps," gets comfort through the Lord's Prayer. "Beautiful, yet simple, easily understood," he writes, the Lord's Prayer "has cleared up finally, for me, much that has been difficult in the Twelve Steps." One member found his spiritual path in quite a different direction: "AA has room for everybody—including those of us who are still wrestling with their unbelief," writes Chris S. in his article "I Don't Need to Understand." "I found that I needed to return to my Native American roots and strengthen my connection with the Great Spirit."

In the story "Stronger & Brighter," B.K., an oldtimer, writes about learning to cherish prayer and meditation. They have "enlarged my heart," B.K. writes. "The quality of my prayer life makes me much more effective in working with other alkies," adding "My intention is to practice, practice and practice, until they throw dirt over me one day."

A Deeper Look
November 2017

W ho knows where having an open mind can lead? My AA story began with a spiritual experience, although I didn't really recognize it at the time. It was November 1979. My best drinking buddy had just gone back to the Marines after a month-long party. My life was a shambles and I was taking a long walk in the park trying to figure out how to pick up the pieces again. I thought about my drinking and the consequences it had brought me.

I'll have to cut back, I told myself. But I realized I couldn't cut back. So I made a monumental decision, one that felt like chopping off an arm: I'll have to quit. But I knew I couldn't do that either. I had already tried limiting my drinking to weekends, trying to prove to myself and others that I could do it. But each of these efforts ended in failure and I found an excuse to drink—and drink heavily.

Without knowing it, I had taken the first half of the First Step while on my walk. For a few moments, I had been given the gift of self-honesty. I saw that I couldn't stop drinking on my own. As I walked along with that realization, something unexplainable happened. I heard a voice within, a deep, kind, resonant voice. It said, "Why not try AA?" All of a sudden, I felt a wave of peace wash over me, accompanied by a sense of excitement. And just a few hours later, I went to my first AA meeting.

In later years, I characterized what happened that day as, "God picking me up and pushing me through the doors of AA." But lasting sobriety didn't come right away. Maybe my Higher Power realized that I couldn't handle too much direct intervention at one time, so he just handed me off to our beloved "group of drunks" and let nature take its course. Thankfully, I felt like I belonged at that first meeting, and so, despite further experiments with controlled drinking, I kept coming back to AA.

My attitude didn't make it easy to get sober. Many AA people approached me, but I kept them at arm's length. I didn't want anyone to know me or get involved in my life. And I had a strong negative reaction to hearing the word "God" in meetings. At the time, I was very prejudiced against religion. Although I had known and admired a few religious people, I never made any connection between their admirable qualities and the beliefs they professed. Religion in general seemed to be a harsh, unsmiling business, full of rules (rules always made me want to rebel) and condemnations. I couldn't understand why otherwise intelligent-seeming people would believe that stuff. So the spiritual aspects of the AA program at first seemed impossible to me.

Fortunately, AA had seen me coming and had an answer ready. Step meetings were a huge help. The words of the Steps always assured me that I could believe in a Higher Power of my own understanding. I didn't have to adopt or agree with anyone else's conception of God. And I learned to keep it simple. I became willing and able to believe that there was a benevolent Higher Power who worked through AA to keep drunks sober. The evidence for that was, at first, in the sober AAs around me. Later, I saw it in my own sobriety.

As time went on, my outright prejudice lessened. I still couldn't see organized religion as anything attractive (or useful) to me, but I could accept it in other people without completely looking down my nose at them. So for several years, my spirituality was based solely on AA principles (as I understood them). That was plenty for me.

But as I progressed in sobriety, I began to feel a need for more. More of what I wasn't exactly sure. The Eleventh Step in the "Twelve and Twelve" told me that for meditation and prayer, "the world's libraries and places of worship are a treasure trove for all seekers." That Step went on to say, "It is to be hoped that every AA who has a religious connection which emphasizes meditation will return to the practice of that devotion as never before."

And the various statements that I had seen from religious leaders, assuring believers that AA would not conflict with their religion, gave me some comfort that the reverse would also be true: that religion would not necessarily conflict with my AA either. Yet I was still puzzled. What could religion offer me?

About this time (year 10 in sobriety), a couple from my AA home group invited me to join a group they were hosting on the Twelve Steps. For 16 weeks, we would meet and go through the Steps using AA literature and other resources. Our group was a mixed one: each of us was in AA or Al-Anon or some combination of a Twelve Step program. The group leader, Dick, a retired professor who had become a counselor, was a long-term "double winner" in two fellowships. So was Margaret, his partner.

I felt that I had worked the Steps before, but this was different. Now I was working them with others, in order (taking two weeks for some of them), doing "homework" and reporting back to the group. Interestingly, the differences in our stories and our backgrounds proved to be one of the group's strengths. Our differences helped us get past the superficial details of our compulsions. We found common ground. Our sharing promoted self-honesty and insight. After working the Steps with this group, my insides felt right with God and the world.

Not long after this experience, I took a two-week trip to stay with friends in Japan. We visited many beautiful, peaceful Buddhist and Shinto shrines, places that persisted in their ancient meditative quiet, as though they were set in a world apart from the nearby bustle of the Japanese cities.

While visiting one of these, I recalled a time when I was drawn to an old painting in a Jesuit retreat house. I remembered how that painting had made me realize that for hundreds of years, other people had been doing just what I was doing at the retreat: purposefully pursuing a relationship with God. I considered how, as a recovering alcoholic, I had something in common with all alcoholics in AA.

But that wasn't all. I had something in common with the Jesuit in the old painting and with the Japanese people who built the shrines.

Though our understandings varied, all of us were seeking a relationship with a Higher Power. I also realized that I didn't have to go far in my search. If I was willing to set aside my old prejudices, there was plenty of opportunity for meaningful prayer and meditation within my own religious tradition.

That idea stayed with me after I returned from Japan. Later that summer, I mulled it over while driving past miles of forest and farms on the way from my home in eastern Ontario to visit family in northern Michigan. It was a beautiful day, sunny and warm. Thanks to my recent experience working the Steps, I was newly unburdened from much of my old baggage and my old lies. I felt clean and true. Admiring the scenery, a deep peace came over me and it stayed.

In the afternoon, I stopped to take a quick dip in a sheltered bay of Lake Superior. It seemed like a bit of paradise. Proceeding onward, I came to a sign for a Catholic shrine, where I felt (and heeded) a strong desire to stop and pray.

Praying at the shrine just felt like the right thing to do. I had so much gratitude to express. After I left, the peaceful feeling and prayerful impulse that drew me there remained with me for many days. Even as it slowly passed, I still felt drawn to pray, and not only in nature, which had been my house of worship for many years, but in (of all places) church.

At the time, I understood that I'd had a powerful spiritual experience, one that the Steps had made me ready for. And it led me, directly and unmistakably, to a religious tradition and practice that I had misunderstood and angrily rejected in my youth.

That experience happened nearly 25 years ago. But to this day, I can still feel its echoes. A new door was opened. The spiritual path presented to me was one that for centuries, millions of faith-seeking and faith-living people had walked. I didn't have to do it all on my own. So I stepped out onto that path, took it seriously and stuck with it. I accepted right away what I could and left the rest on the shelf for later, just as I had done in AA.

Today, I feel fortunate in being able to participate in a religious service on my lunch hour nearly every weekday, as well as on Sundays. The practice of my religion strengthens my AA program, while my experience of powerlessness and humility and amends and forgiveness in AA infuses a deep personal meaning into my religion. They work hand in hand.

It's not uncommon to hear disparaging comments about religion in AA meetings. I don't know if I ever made any myself, but I definitely used to feel that way. That's why I wanted to write about my spiritual journey in AA. This is just my story. I hope it doesn't offend anyone. I'm not advocating for any particular religion. Nor am I saying that everybody needs to have one. It surprised me to discover that I did.

In my case, I would have missed out on so much that is good if I had hung onto my old resentments and prejudices and my self-satisfied attitude of "contempt prior to investigation." Step Two in the "Twelve and Twelve" says, "AAs tread innumerable paths in their quest for faith" and tells us "you'll be sure to discover one that suits if only you look and listen."

Mike S.
Whitehouse, Ohio

Prayer
January 1980

The AA program only suggests that newcomers attempt to begin to conceive of a power greater than themselves, in their own individual terms. After that, an oldtimer might suggest to a skeptical newcomer—along with not picking up the first drink—faking prayer and keeping an open mind.

I came into this program a drunken atheist. Today, I pray. My being sober is a reflection of the good attributes of some Higher Power; it is not a reflection of any moral virtue or strength of will on my part.

This change in a drunken, hardcore, cynical atheist is a miracle beyond human comprehension. However, one aspect of the program has always been required for me to remain sober—results. Prayer works. If prayer didn't work and show results, I'd become an atheist again today.

Spirituality happens to be extremely practical. Prayer, reading the AA literature, going to meetings, using the Steps and helping another alcoholic all combine to make my life easier and more comfortable, hour to hour, day to day.

As an atheist, I faked prayer on a trial basis in the beginning. The results have altered my viewpoint of the cosmos. An unseen realm does exist. I do not attend church, nor have I experienced a spiritual awakening; I'm still a fire-breathing cynic. Yet I pray regularly to something unseen and so vast that I, as a human being, can never understand or even name it.

I pray because of the positive results that flow from prayer. I'm a pragmatist. So for today, I have become an agnostic who occasionally experiences violent swings toward faith. With all the blessings that have been bestowed upon me in a year and a half, I still experience doubts and have not made that quantum leap to faith.

All this proves only one thing: that some nuts are tougher to crack than others. Today, I'm still faking prayer and getting results. Maybe God likes nuts, especially the hard ones.

R. E.
Philadelphia, Pennsylvania

Into the Woods
September 2007

I see now how the Twelve Steps can work upside down. In early sobriety, as I began to work the Steps, each new day I felt like I was climbing up the "ladder of success." I had found, and now belonged in, the human race. It was wonderful. I was making sober friends and life was getting easier without alcohol in it.

Six months into the program, I was given a blessing. My Higher

Power put a mother and her baby into my life. I felt that God had given me the chance to do for another what I hadn't been able to do for my own daughter.

At one of the meetings I attended, there was a woman who had lost her child to the child welfare system. The conditions to get the baby back were for her to find a babysitter, a job, and a home for her and the baby. I had just lost a job and, without hesitation, I volunteered to babysit. What a wonderful gift I was given. I loved and cared for this baby as I wasn't able to do for my own. I felt that God was giving me a second chance to be a mother. I had this baby day and night and I fell in love with her, feeling like this would go on forever. But the day came, months later, when I was no longer needed in their lives.

As long as things were going my way, I was in conformance with God's will; when they changed, it was back to my will. I fell down the ladder of the Twelve Steps. Fortunately, I stopped at the First Step—I didn't drink. I reverted back to my old self-will run riot though. I was in a rage, and the old thinking was back in full-force. I wanted to call children and youth services and tell them stories about the mother. How dare she take this child from me? I was an emotional mess again. I had forgotten two things: singleness of purpose and God's will for us.

I called other women in the program and they talked and walked me through the rage. They met me at meetings, they supported me—not in my thinking, but in my emotional breakdown. They kept me sober and active in AA. One day, I was finally sick and tired of the pain. I picked up the "Twelve and Twelve" and went out into the woods just to be alone and try to practice what I had been hearing in the rooms of Alcoholics Anonymous. "Resentment is the 'number one' offender." I knew I had to let go of this somehow. I made the decision to stay in the woods until I was relieved of this terrible resentment and the pain it was causing me.

I opened the book and it happened to fall on the Eleventh Step. I started reading, if for no other reason than to stop thinking of the hate and hurt I was feeling. I came to the St. Francis Prayer. I followed the direction it gave, going back again and again to reread the prayer, trying to get its inner essence. I didn't give up. In between, I asked God to please help me find relief from my alcoholism. I read the Step again.

I don't know how many times I read the prayer, or how long I was in the woods, but the last time I read it, it was as if a light went on. The very first line of the prayer hit me: "Lord, make me a channel of thy peace—that where there is hatred, I may bring love..." These were life-saving words for me. I realized that God's will for me was to be a channel. I was put in place to help a mother and daughter come back together, the way it was supposed to be.

God did for me what no human power could. I went into the woods feeling hate, pain and despair. I came out feeling love, peace and serenity. The power of prayer was a beautiful lesson to have learned from the Fellowship of Alcoholics Anonymous.

Peg S.
Panama City, Florida

Finds Lord's Prayer Key to Steps
September 1946

Just recently, after more than four years on the ball in AA, several of the 12 Steps were made simple and clear to me by a new approach. The light that clarified these Steps for me may appeal to some beginners who, like myself, find the program in its entirety hard to take.

Four years ago last February Jimmy B. caught me between drinks, after a post-graduate course at Samaritan Institute. I thought at first my name was on the sucker list—there must be a dotted line somewhere in the offing. But my curiosity was aroused, and I knew something had to be done about my drinking.

From occasional drunken sprees in 1916 to continuous drinking and frequent spells of complete disability (hospitalized twice because of uremic convulsions followed by DTs; hospitalized for attempted suicide; failure of the Samaritan cure in 1940 and 1941; loss of two businesses and innumerable jobs; divorced once and on the brink again), February 1941 found me desperately seeking an answer—so I attended my first AA meeting.

That meeting convinced me that this was it; the people I met had regained health, stability, self respect and a place in the community. If it worked for them it must and would for me. I went home filled with enthusiasm and elation. But one nagging doubt, a real fear, assailed me. Which of the 12 Steps must I subscribe to and which must I practice? What of all this spiritual approach; the requirement that I acknowledge and turn my life over to God? Those were staggering thoughts.

I told my wife about the meeting and my hope that it was finally a way out for me. Then I went out to the park to thrash out alone the need to accept God. And I knew I could never hurdle those Steps. For years I'd vainly called on God to help me. (I know now that I'd actually attempted to trade with God—only when in a very bad trading position). There was much to think about, so I wound up in the rear booth of a taproom. Not to drink, of course. It was cold in the park and I needed to be alone with my thoughts. That was Thursday night.

Fortunately I sobered up enough by Saturday morning to remember mention of a downtown clubhouse, quite near where I lived. Somehow I found it—and the answer to my problem.

Jimmy B. arrived soon after I did. He and several other members told me to forget about the 12 Steps—to skip the "God part" of the program. "If you're sure of the First Step, hang onto that. Stick around here awhile with an open mind. Anything you don't like, just skip it. And remember, easy does it."

So I stuck around there, a few hours every day. Attended all meetings, went on calls and visited alcoholics in the psychopathic wards of the city hospital. There was just one reservation in my mind. I'd not be a hypocrite by reciting the Lord's Prayer when I couldn't subscribe to a word of it. Of course I rose with the others—it would be too conspicuous to remain seated—and with gritted teeth remained silent.

I couldn't help hearing that prayer; hearing it spoken in frank sincerity by a group of people who had suffered all the reverses that had plagued me. Sometime during the first few weeks I began to follow the prayer as I heard it; to think it and think about it. Within a year I was saying it aloud at meetings and meaning every word of it.

For over three years I've had a comfortable feeling of peace and serenity. Some of the AA Steps have remained high hurdles, perhaps through that early habit of thought regarding them. Then a few weeks ago at a meeting the Steps were discussed in a way that started a new train of thought. After several days it dawned on me that I'd accepted those toughest Steps some three years ago. I'd found comfort in the Lord's Prayer. I'd been thinking and saying it—and meaning it. I could start with "Our Father who art in Heaven" and end with "for Thine is the kingdom and the power"—and there was Step 2.

"Thy will be done" is certainly Step 3.

"Forgive us our trespasses... and lead us not into temptation, but deliver us from evil" was a way of practicing Steps 6 and 7.

And when the Lord's Prayer has been uttered sincerely and humbly, Step 11 has truly been accepted.

The Lord's Prayer, beautiful yet simple, easily understood, has cleared up finally for me much that has been difficult in the 12 Steps of AA.

Bill C.
Philadelphia, Pennsylvania

As the Spirit Moves Us
February 2021

For three years meetings, working the Steps with my sponsor and service had kept me sober. I thought I was doing pretty good. I even reached the point where I was about 97% certain a Higher Power existed.

My concept of a Higher Power did not come as the white flash variety. It was more of an intellectual reasoning still in progress. In fact, the only real disappointment in my sobriety was that I hadn't been asked to sponsor another alcoholic.

But now I was going on a four-day trip up to a wilderness area without meetings, phone service or contact with anyone in recovery. I just knew I was going to drink. I wasn't going to give in easily though. I calculated I'd be able to white-knuckle it for at least two days before the compulsion overran me. Then would begin the process of destroying the repaired relationships with my family, ruining my regained health and letting down the people in my home group. I knew alcohol would win.

I had just flown to Minneapolis, rented a car, and driven three hours north to join one of my dearest, longtime friends on a dogsledding/camping/ice fishing trip near the Canadian border. Early the next morning, six other guys I had never met were going to show up at my friend's isolated farm with their sleds and dog teams to join us for the drive up to the Boundary Waters Wilderness Area. Wall tents with little stoves and good down sleeping bags would keep us warm at night. And for sure there would be plenty of alcohol. After all, what do a bunch of guys do around a campfire at 20 below zero if not get drunk?

When I arrived at my friend's, we visited in his small kitchen, while outside an icy wind battered the old farmhouse. His wife, a gourmet cook, fixed dinner. They already had a buzz from several glasses of wine. Delicious smells filled the air. What a perfectly snug, cozy scene. Then the sudden thought came to me: Why can't I be part of this warm, loving picture?

That simple thought is all it took. The craving for alcohol hit me full force. My mind spun a hundred miles an hour. In confusion bordering on panic, I excused myself and went into the living room and sat in an old easy chair next to a table stacked with a hodgepodge of magazines and newspapers. I thought of calling my sponsor back in Montana while I still had the chance, but there was no cell service at the farm, and I didn't want my friends to overhear me on their landline in the kitchen. I was afraid they'd think I was "weak." Part of me knew that was a poor excuse, but the alcoholic part resisted it.

Twice before, in early sobriety, I'd faced irresistible cravings. It felt literally like a hand was pulling me toward the liquor store. I was still pretty allergic to the "God with a capitol G" word at the time. In fact, even the word "prayer" made me uncomfortable. Both times I managed to mumble a brief prayer and the craving went away. But deep in my mind, I figured it could possibly just have been some sort of "self-hypnosis" instead of an actual Higher Power. That left me enough wiggle room to avoid total surrender.

Sitting in my friend's easy chair with nowhere else to turn and fueled by desperation, I tried to think of the "right" words to go into a prayer. My thoughts whirled in fragments and nothing came together. I finally whispered something like, "Higher Power, this is Jake here. Please take away my compulsion to drink." That really sounded dumb. It couldn't possibly work. But it was the best I could do.

I waited skeptically for a minute or two, but no message came. The prayer hadn't worked. I wasn't surprised. In frustration and growing despair, the idea came to me to flip through the magazines stacked on the table and maybe I'd find a "sign" from God. I opened some up, but I was so upset and confused I couldn't concentrate. I grabbed an old newspaper, but the headlines just irritated me. As I slapped the paper down, ready to give up, my eye caught something near the bottom of the pile. For some reason I decided to tug it out and see what it was. Anything to delay the inevitable.

I pulled out a one-page newsletter put together by a local grocery store/gas station. At the top were the words, "Published as often as the spirit moves us." In the top right corner, in small letters was written, "Freedom is not free." I scanned down to see some announcements, such as a church ice cream social, a wedding and a birth announcement. I thought about the church social. This stupid newsletter seemed to be mocking me. One of the resentments in my Fourth Step was groups of seemingly cheerful people visiting in front of a church after services. In my drinking days, those people really ticked me off. I figured they were either total hypocrites or stupid sheep believing anything they were told.

As I put aside the newsletter, a feeling I can only describe as an almost unbearable soul sickness settled over me. My last chance was the God thing, and it hadn't worked. Now I was about to return to that dark, pitiful feeling of worthlessness, and I was powerless to stop myself. I would go back into the kitchen and try to pretend everything was alright. Fake it. I had been pretty good at that the last few years of my drinking.

But I glanced at the newsletter a final time and caught the word "happiness" in a heading at the bottom. Sort of like a robot without its own will, I began to read. By the time I was halfway through, actual goose bumps ran up my arms.

It read: "WHAT, THEN, IS HAPPINESS? The answer is not complex. Happiness is simply a state of inner freedom. Freedom from what? With a bit of self-insight, every individual can answer that question for himself. It is freedom from the secret angers and anxieties we tell no one about. It is freedom from muddled thinking that drives us to compulsive actions, and later, to regrets. It is freedom from painful cravings that deceive us into thinking that our attainment of this person or of that circumstance will make everything right. Happiness is liberty from everything that makes us unhappy. –Author Unknown."

All of a sudden, a profound calmness washed over me. The fear that I was going to drink totally vanished. I sat in awe. My Creator had chosen the perfect way to answer my prayer. The words could not possibly have been more specific to my situation. This was no accident. God had done for me what I couldn't do for myself. At that moment I became 100% certain a Higher Power existed. I'd never have to feel alone again.

I returned to the kitchen to join my friends. Love for them and the world began to radiate through me. Everything seemed good. I asked if I could keep the little newsletter and they said sure.

The guys who showed up early the next morning with their dog teams and sleds turned out to be great people. A couple of biologists, a special education teacher, people like that. And alcohol? On the last night of the trip, one of the biologists brought out a single pint of whiskey and passed it around the fire, the only liquor I saw on the whole trip. Two of the guys joined him for a sip and the bottle went home still three-fourths full. How does that happen?

Within a week after I returned to my home group in Montana, a man asked me to sponsor him. It was obvious that I hadn't been ready the three years before. I had overlooked my intellectual pride as a character defect. The Higher Power knows what it's doing. I don't.

That Northern Minnesota dogsledding trip happened 15 years ago. I still carry that well-worn newsletter folded in my billfold and still get goosebumps whenever I take it out and share it with another alcoholic. The Higher Power that answered my prayer that night has kept me sober and useful through the tragedy of addicted family members, the ups and downs of relationships and periods of self-doubt. It has also been with me for many rewarding hours of service work, fun with friends and the profound blessing of simply being alive and experiencing whatever life throws at me, both good and bad. I still sponsor the man who asked me when I returned from Minnesota. Or maybe he sponsors me. It's getting a little cloudy in that respect. We laugh about it.

There's a passage in the Big Book that defines my spiritual condition before I sat in my Minnesota friend's easy chair all those years ago:

"We were grateful that Reason had brought us so far. But somehow, we couldn't quite step ashore. Perhaps we had been leaning too heavily on reason that last mile and we did not like to lose our support."

I reached out in desperation and my Creator was there for me. And later in the chapter, it says:

"The barriers he had built through the years were swept away....He had stepped from the bridge to shore. For the first time, he lived in conscious companionship with his Creator."

Since that trip to Northern Minnesota, I have never had a craving for alcohol again.

Jake H.
Whitefish, Montana

Many Steps to Prayer
November 2018

The speaker at my first AA meeting was a man named Harold. That was 33 years ago. I don't remember much of what he said, but one thing stuck in my mind: He described alcoholism as a threefold illness of body, mind and spirit. That made immediate sense to me.

I came to AA at age 45, but emotionally and spiritually I was still a stunted teenager. I had to start growing up. Physically, I was very sick. After my last drinking bout, I tried to kill myself and was rushed to the hospital. I was so weak when I was discharged that I had to use a cane and was too ill to go to the AA meeting I was invited to that night by the two men who Twelfth Stepped me.

Mentally, there was clearly something terribly wrong with me. I felt so abandoned and terrified of life that the only solution was suicide. I didn't want to die, but didn't know how to live. Spiritually, I was hollow inside.

When I was a teenager, I was intensely religious. I belonged to a Pentecostal church and preached in gospel halls, at Speakers' Corner in London's Hyde Park and to holiday seaside crowds. At age 17, I told my father he would burn in the flames of hell unless he was saved by Jesus. But then I was called up for national service in the Royal Air Force and was sent a long way from home and I found another "holy spirit," known as alcohol.

When I got drunk for the first time, I had a counterfeit spiritual experience. I experienced limitless expansion in my mind. I became a spiritual space explorer. I worshipped alcohol, but it proved a false, unfaithful god. Disguised as a benign Higher Power, alcohol actually sought my destruction.

After 25 years of uncontrollable drinking, I reached that state of "pitiful and incomprehensible demoralization" that the Big Book describes. I reached the jumping off point. I wished for the end.

The chapter, "Working With Others" in the Big Book points out that our prospect's "religious education and training may be far superior to yours." That applied to me the night I was Twelfth Stepped by those two AA members, a former bank executive and an unemployed laborer.

Among many attempts to control my drinking, I'd left a job where I faced dismissal because of my drunken irresponsibility and then I decided to train as a teacher. At university, I received a commendation from an examiner for an essay that I wrote comparing and contrasting the apocalyptic millenarianism of the synoptic gospels with the eschatology of the fourth gospel. Along with Christianity, I studied Hinduism and Judaism and I graduated with a qualification to teach religion.

Yes, I had academic religious credentials and letters after my name, but the men who Twelfth Stepped me were sober and I could not stop drinking. My problem was not lack of religious knowledge. My problem, the Big Book tells me, was lack of power.

Years later, when I was secretary of an AA Step group, I heard a member say he was a doctor of divinity. I asked him to share on the Eleventh Step. I said that being a doctor of divinity would give him a flying start on the topic. "The exact opposite," he told me. "With my superior religious knowledge and church attendance, I thought, What could I learn from a bunch of housewives, plumbers and bankers? My intellectual arrogance kept me drinking. It was only when I was absolutely beaten that I realized the difference between religious knowledge and church attendance and the spirituality of sobriety."

By the time I went to my first AA meeting, I'd turned my back on religion and was a skeptical, quarrelsome agnostic. The mention of God in the Steps and Traditions, however, did not deter me. I went to that meeting a week after a determined suicide attempt and had become as "open-minded to conviction and willing to listen as the dying can be," as it says in *Twelve Steps and Twelve Traditions*. I'd become "ready to do anything which will lift the merciless obsession" with alcohol. I had to "resign from the debating society" and become willing to accept advice and live experimentally.

I suffered terribly from neurotic anxiety in early recovery and said the Serenity Prayer like a mantra to get me through. Later, I adopted my own silent meditation: "Love's will not mine, be still and know." I repeated this continually until it became internalized. I repeat it while out walking my dog.

In 1952, when he was 27 years sober, Bill W. wrote in Grapevine, "Whenever I find myself under acute tensions, I lengthen my daily walks and slowly repeat our Serenity Prayer in rhythm to my steps and breathing.... This benign healing process of repetition...has seldom failed to restore me to at least a workable emotional balance." It works for me, too, because I still have psychological hangups and neurotic tendencies. Today, I know a drink won't solve them.

The Big Book says, "Be quick to see where religious people are right. Make use of what they offer," and, "Not all of us join religious bodies, but most of us favor such memberships." The AA group I joined met at a Quaker meeting house. I was intrigued by a poster I saw on their notice board, so I went to a Quaker meeting one Sunday and I've been going ever since. In recovery, I began attending spiritual retreats and quiet days organized by AA members. The first retreat I went to at a convent was an ordeal. I wasn't long sober and found it almost impossible to talk to other members. At mealtimes, I sat with my head bowed over my plate, avoiding eye contact.

Later, I overcame my fears and began to organize and lead retreats and quiet days myself. Some years ago, my sponsor suggested I might find weekly Christian meditation sessions helpful. When the nuns who organized them moved, my wife and I agreed to lead the group.

The Eleventh Step is about our growing relationship with God. I am profoundly grateful that long ago, atheist member Jimmy B. insisted that the qualification "as we understood Him" be added to the Third and Eleventh Steps. The phrase is italicized to emphasize its importance.

Today, I am a reverent, open-minded agnostic. AA does not require me to believe in a transcendent, metaphysical being to stay sober. When I pray, I believe I connect with that "unsuspected inner resource" and "great reality" deep within me, which the Big Book talks about. It is that source of power greater than my ego-self which I accessed when I admitted to my innermost self that I was an alcoholic.

To me, as the Bible says, God is love. Each morning, I ask to be shown the loving way ahead. I ask to be able to help another alcoholic and I always add, "If it be your will." Every time I enter an AA meeting, it is an act of prayer. I'm saying, "I can't do this on my own. I need help." Attentive listening to other members when they share is also a form of meditation because it takes my magnifying mind off me.

In that June 1958 Grapevine article, Bill W. wrote, "The other Steps can keep most of us sober and somehow functioning. But Step Eleven can keep us growing, if we try hard and work at it continually."

That has been true in my own experience. As the member whose story is called, "The Keys of the Kingdom," in the Big Book wrote, "We must have a program for living that allows for limitless expansion."

Anonymous

Stronger & Brighter
November 2015

As I approach my 76th anniversary of life and my 47th of sobriety, I'm excited. I'm compelled to share about our awesome Step Eleven. It's really something how the slow, steady progress of this Step pays dividends of happiness.

How did this happen to a falling-down drunk like me? I believe sponsorship and persistence were the keys. One day early in sobriety, after I had asked for the grace not to drink, I was challenged to spend a minute or two in the morning in prayer. Then I was asked to cherish this good habit—and persist, no matter what—every day. I was also told to pray more seriously and spend more time at it.

The result was similar to going to AA meetings: I reached a point where I crossed a line and a hunger developed in me for more. I knew I had to do this to stay sober. But having to do it, and wanting to do it, are a world apart. When the fire is lit inside and given TLC, the fire grows stronger and the light grows brighter.

Yes, there are dry times when I feel no connection. But I just persist and take an inventory of myself (not of others). Then I make sure that there are no amends I need to make, or other forms of conduct that are the product of untreated alcoholism. If I do all these things, my HP connection always returns. (By the way, I can always come up with a list of rationalizations a foot long of why I shouldn't spend the time in prayer and meditation. I have experienced most of them and can tell you that, like all half-measures, they are pure BS.)

I've now developed deep personal convictions of right and wrong based on experience—error and pain being my best teachers. When trying my best to follow these convictions, I have a strong sense of being linked with my Higher Power. My faith and trust in God has strengthened manyfold as a result. I love it when I'm centered in the Higher Power and my program, and remember to prioritize my values, which are often at odds with those of the world. When I'm in harmony with my values, I'm calm and at peace. Good stuff! And I see no limits to my personal spiritual growth as I continue to practice this learned good habit.

The biggest payoff of all is that prayer and meditation have enlarged my heart. By that, I mean my capacity to love God, my alkie brothers and sisters, my family and all of God's children. That's a wonderful feeling of internal peace and happiness that I did not think could be sustained. But it's the fourth dimension of which our AA founders spoke—and that's priceless.

Prayer and meditation are time spent with my HP, which gave me the gift of sobriety. I have zero power and God has all power. When I asked (begged) God, he gave me an entirely different life—a life where the moral high road is the goal each day, a life with a way to get back up when I run off the main road. That's the life that my creator, who loves me and watches over me, wants for me. I'm grateful to my alcoholism for getting my attention so I could approach him and surrender to live.

Today, I have two periods of quiet time: one in the A.M. and another one in the P.M. Each lasts usually about 45 minutes. And I strive to pray continuously between those times, with prayers for people special to me and for knowledge of what he wants me to do. All those random thoughts that run through my head during my waking hours can be focused with a lot of practice. My intention is to practice, practice and practice, until they throw dirt over me one day.

And boy, does it have benefits. This is not goody-two-shoes stuff. It's practical thinking that keeps me protected from the daily war with untreated alcoholism. The quality of my prayer life makes me much more effective in working with other alkies. In fact, it's directly proportionate to it. His will for me is to pass on the good news of my experience with all 12 Steps. In doing that, I'm lifted to this fourth dimension, where I'm relatively happy, no matter what my life circumstances. That's a blessing for this ex-drunk. I think I'll try to stay sober one more day.

B. K.
Grove City, Ohio

I Don't Need to Understand
November 2020

I have been a subscriber to Grapevine since I got sober in AA. My sponsor got me a subscription for Christmas, which is a policy I continue with my own sponsees. I was reading a member's story recently, and his struggle with the Higher Power moved me to write.

In all my years in AA (in four different states, speaking two different languages) I have never heard anyone criticized for identifying themselves as atheist or agnostic or for talking openly about having trouble with their concept of a Higher Power. I've always encountered a warm acceptance from everyone in AA, whatever religious tradition they were coming from. I always felt a friendly reassurance that, as I often hear in meetings, this is a spiritual, not a religious program. You don't have to believe in anything, and you can use AA itself as a Higher Power.

I came into AA still bitter against what I had experienced of organized religion. I had only seen religion misused in hypocritical ways. In our Fellowship, I learned to both respect and appreciate that many people can find their spiritual inspiration and guidance in ways that don't work for me.

In my own search for spirituality, I found that I needed to return to my Native American roots and strengthen my connection with the Great Spirit. I have no trouble using other religions' words for the same thing: God, Allah, Buddha, or whatever works for each individual. I've come to realize that the people who wrote our original AA literature simply used the Christian language of their upbringing—although many, (including our cofounder Bill W.) had rejected "God" and "religion" themselves at some point.

Let me share one thing I've learned from my own journey since getting sober in AA: When we are truly comfortable with ourselves, and what we have or have not experienced of a Higher Power, we feel no need to run down people who see it differently. We no longer try to mend our insecurities with negative comparisons between others and ourselves. We have no need to criticize atheists or those inclined to spend time on their knees praying for divine protection. We don't need to pick apart other AA members' understanding of atheism or agnosticism or faith.

What's more, we don't attempt to nominate specific human beings (including the Commandant of the Marine Corps, to cite one example I've heard) as a Higher Power for AA. Human beings simply can't handle the job.

Instead, we can turn to a vital ingredient of AA—humility. I was taught by AA oldtimers that humility means "being right-sized." Or, as one member wrote in the Big Book story "The Man Who Mastered

Fear": "The scales had dropped from my eyes, and I could see life in its proper perspective. I had tried to be the center of my own little world, whereas God was the center of a vast universe of which I was perhaps an essential, but a very tiny, part."

We don't have to call it "God." We don't have to have a word for it. AA has room for everybody—including those of us who are still wrestling with their unbelief.

It's OK that we human beings can't parse it all out intellectually. Look, gophers and earthworms don't understand nuclear physics. They don't need to. They do their jobs aerating and fertilizing our Mother Earth so she can grow the plants we all depend on. Similarly, I don't understand our Higher Power. I don't need to. All I know is that one evening, when I was really at the end of my rope, I looked into the universe and said, "I could never 'believe in God' like folks say you're supposed to, but if there is anybody or anything there who cares whether I live or die, I sure wish you'd let me know."

Something very wonderful did respond to my call. I choose to call that something or someone the Great Spirit. So I do my job. I stay sober today. I clean house. I help others.

Chris S.
Hillsboro, Oregon

The Answer to My Prayer
September 2019

My sponsor taught me to pray. He started me off with the simplest prayer: "Help." He called it the intellectual's prayer because I could say it and still reserve my right not to believe in God. I didn't even have to use the word "God," just that one essential word. He asked, since I thought of myself as an intellectual, if I thought I could memorize it. OK wise guy, I memorized it.

The first time I used this one-word prayer I wanted a drink so badly it physically hurt all the way through my chest and abdomen.

The prayer worked. I stopped wanting a drink. I stopped hurting. My muscles relaxed. The prayer had a measurable external, physical result.

I began to be convinced of the power of prayer. I still wasn't sure there was anything out there that I was actually praying to, but I started adding my own words to the prayer a little at a time. "Me" got tacked on right away. Later, I would begin with "Please." The day I said, "Please help me do the right thing," marked a major shift out of my self-centered attitude.

Even so, I was having trouble believing in anything "greater than myself." I couldn't tell what invisible beings might be lurking around the corner in my paranoid delusions or what benevolent angels might be fighting them off. I didn't know if there was one loving God at the helm of the universe or a gigantic monster driving us all deeper into hell.

So my sponsor told me to pray to believe whatever is true. Whatever true is, whatever it turns out to be, I prayed, let me believe that.

I began that night and continued into the next day. I repeated the prayer all day long whenever I thought of it. I didn't have much of anything else to think about. I said it as a mantra, constantly throughout the day, no matter what else I was doing.

My desperate prayer calmed me in the midst of the day's ups and downs. It sustained me through my low-skill, low-thought, recovery-focused job and through the walk to my AA meeting in the evening. I began to gain confidence that I might actually learn something from praying, but I still didn't have a clue as to what that might be.

I sat in the meeting still repeating the prayer quietly to myself. One guy shared about his struggle with suicidal thoughts, which shook me out of my private reverie. He said he was seriously considering doing it that day. The meeting leader suggested that he read some particular passage in the Big Book. The guy said he didn't have a book. The leader delicately moved the discussion to the next member of the group on whatever that day's topic was and the suicidal guy sat there quietly until the end of the meeting.

After the meeting, the leader spoke with the suicidal guy. The group secretary interrupted them to offer the man a Big Book. The man said, "You don't understand. I don't have any money." Indeed, he had mentioned that as one of the problems that was driving him to kill himself.

"You don't understand," said the secretary. "We want to give this to you. The group wants you to have it." And the secretary handed the book over to him. The guy took it.

I sat there repeating my little prayer while watching all of this. No one was paying attention to me but I was paying close attention to them. They were playing out the answer to my prayer.

It suddenly occurred to me that even if this was all a hallucination, somewhere in the universe there existed this kind of love. Pure love, no strings attached, caring for another human being just because they need it. Giving someone the very thing that will help in the situation they're in.

Love. I can believe in love. That's the answer to my prayer.

Thomas G.
Silver Springs, Maryland

CHAPTER THREE

Getting There Through Action

Practicing a spiritual connection while running,
exercising, swimming and more

A s it says in the Step Two chapter of the AA book *Twelve Steps and Twelve Traditions*, "AAs tread innumerable paths in their quest for faith." For many of the writers sharing their experience, strength and hope in this chapter, that pathway was marked by a broad range of activities, from yoga and swimming to bike riding and skateboarding. For these alcoholics such activities offer an entry point for the spirit—a portal to spiritual awareness and experience.

"We are told to turn our lives and our wills over to a Higher Power," writes J.J., a former swimming instructor in his story "To Sink...Or Swim?" "How simple that became for me to understand when I compared it to relying on the buoyancy of water, a power that is always there, ever available to us merely by our acceptance of it, by our relaxing into it, not striving for it, not searching for it, just being willing to accept it." And bike rider B.B. in "Back in the Saddle Again," shares that there are three secret rules for bike riding that you won't find in any bike books: "Easy does it. One day at a time. Keep coming back."

Prayer and meditation can always be further developed and using these practices regularly can build spiritual resources. Developing a set of "spiritual muscles" is a theme shared by many AAs and particularly by Kim H., as illustrated in her story "Sink or Swim." "If I exercise my spiritual muscles daily, keep them strong and ready to respond," she writes, "chances are when I am truly in need, I can engage them to handle any difficulty or challenge I face."

Calm and Quiet
(Excerpt)
November 2019

E ven though I've been sober since 2004, I had struggled to find an Eleventh Step practice that worked for me. I continued to "fake it," hanging on to any tiny example of peace and quiet as my daily meditation. This included basic gardening, the "quiet" five minutes it took me to send out my Daily Reading emails each morning and even washing the dishes.

In the last three years, I played a major role in my failed marriage, a relatively peaceful divorce and a co-parenting solution for our beautiful 5-year-old daughter. This progression, from divorce to a successful parenting partnership, has been influenced greatly by my new, consistent Eleventh Step practice of intense daily yoga.

As a precocious child, I was a real know-it-all and a verbal bully. As an adult drunk, I was scared to death of anything challenging or unknown. I drank my way through restaurant jobs and women, as I ran from Virginia to Texas and back. I do not recommend drunken bus travel for anyone. I can tell you that alcohol withdrawal in a bus bathroom is a real drag.

Liquor finally stomped me into a reasonable state. I could no longer envision life either with or without alcohol. When I came back to the Blue Ridge Mountains of Virginia one last time to drink myself to death, I failed again and ended up sober.

I was guided to the Top of the Mountain AA group and to a gentle, loving sponsor, Irvin. He gently and lovingly told me to "get in the literature and stay in the literature." Irvin has never told me what to do, he simply shows me what to do.

Irvin and I have continued to go through all Twelve Steps. I now guide other men through them, based on his example. One of our Eleventh Step practices is keeping a log of obstacles to meditation.

Lack of time and of willingness were regularly at the top of my list.

Just as drinking had robbed me of the ability to generate the money I needed to drink, calamity forced me to find the time and willingness to get serious about the Eleventh Step. As my unresolved anger pushed my now-ex-wife away, Step work, retreats, prayers and therapy could not stop the destruction of the marriage. When I knew beyond the shadow of a doubt that I needed to "pause, when agitated or doubtful, and ask for the right thought or action," I couldn't do it. I did not have the spiritual resources to shut my stupid mouth when I knew I needed to.

One day, while I was in the bowels of the Information Center where I work, surrounded by super computer clusters, my crazy obstacle-racing coworker and friend invited me to a noon yoga class. Even though the idea of yoga filled me with "contempt prior to investigation," something made me say yes. I soon found myself in a room with a string of prayer flags hanging in the window. There I met a small, strong yoga teacher from Greece, named Lynn.

Teacher Lynn is a deeply invested spiritual seeker. She speaks glowingly of her teacher, her teacher's teacher and her teacher's teacher's teacher, just as I do of my AA sponsorship lineage. She's a stickler for precise and simple hand placement.

The message at my home group is "Keep It Simple," which fits well with our teacher, who doesn't dictate a God or gods we pray to. She leaves that up to us.

In AA I have been granted the latitude to find a Higher Power I can get to know and love. A year and a half ago, I found a home in that class, just as I did when I walked into the Top of the Mountain Group for the first time, broken and battered.

Each day, before our first "om" or "sun salutation," our yoga teacher asks us to set an intention. I choose to focus on my beautiful ex-wife and gift my practice to her. This small consistent action has helped me be a better daddy and a better friend. It has also helped to calm and quiet the unsolicited response.

Jason C.
Fairlawn, Virginia

To Sink...Or Swim?
(Excerpt)
July 1954

When I first came to AA I immediately realized that the members had found something that was far superior to the miserable restlessness and agony of being "on the wagon." I wanted what they had, for I knew that for me to maintain continued sobriety I must find a contented sobriety. I also decided if they could do it I could too.

Although the program was simple, it seemed illusive until I decided to relate it to something with which I was familiar. I'd been a swimming instructor, so I simplified the program for myself and made it understandable and usable by relating it to swimming.

I had been told the Twelve Steps and our many sayings such as "Easy Does It," "Live and Let Live" and our 24-hour program are merely suggestions, that there are no musts. This I could understand, for there are no musts in swimming. It's rather impossible to compel a person to swim or breathe properly. Yet, if he wishes to advance his abilities and his own safety, he can do so only by following the suggestions offered.

There are many swimmers who never learn to breathe properly. Their endurance is short and their safety questionable. Knowing this I decided to follow our Steps and all other suggestions to the best of my ability in order to give myself the greatest possible opportunity for relief from this compulsion I had so long suffered.

The slogan "Easy Does It" fits perfectly: how many times had I told my swimmers "Relax—take it easy"? The mental picture of a swimmer tensely flailing at the water is enough to remind me quickly that "Easy Does It."

With beginners, the first job as an instructor is to gain their confidence. So too, confidence in the sponsor is of prime importance. By the sponsor's story the "pigeon" learns he knows whereof he talks. The beginner has to see others swimming, relaxed and enjoying it, to know it can be done and to desire to learn how. Isn't that pretty much how we, by being at meetings contentedly sober, carry the message to the newcomer? Don't we try to show him it can be done and help him to want to exchange his old life for our new one?

Many have tried tossing people into the water to get them to swim. Seldom does it work except in reverse. The desire must be instilled in the person before he can successfully handle himself in this new environment. So too it is with our program. A willing pupil is an apt pupil.

In all Red Cross swimming they use what is called the "buddy system." Each swimmer, including the advanced ones, at all times has a buddy close at hand. We in AA do likewise. First and foremost is our reliance on a power greater than ourselves, then our sponsor, our telephone therapy and our meetings, where we learn we are no longer alone, we who felt so alone before. These meetings provide an opportunity not only to enjoy the deep feeling of fellowship, but to learn how others work the program. This is similar to the times we used to sit on the shore or a raft watching the other swimmers and learning by their example, as well as by their mistakes, how to improve our own abilities. This is one way to work our Tenth Step.

To swim in comfort and safety we dress, or undress, accordingly and leave behind the many trappings of our old environment.

To live this new life AA offers—a life of sobriety—we also find that for contentment and safety's sake we must discard many of our old hindrances: the negative things with which we approached AA—our fears, dishonesties and self-pity. So we work the Sixth Step, exchanging our old ways of reacting for new, positive ways. We find we seldom can do this immediately, but we are told that a sincere willingness to do so is sufficient to head us in the right direction. As we discard our old attire one garment at a time, so too we'll gradually find ourselves discarding our old burdensome thoughts, replacing them with the simple principles of AA's Twelve Steps.

We are told to turn our lives and our wills over to a Higher Power.

Again, to be willing to do so is sufficient to begin. How simple that became for me to understand when I compared it to relying on the buoyancy of the water, a power that is always there, ever available to us merely by our acceptance of it, by our relaxing into it, not striving for it, not searching for it, just being willing to accept it; a power that is always sufficient for our needs, never changing no matter what depth we find ourselves in, nor whether there be storm or calm. All we have to do is to be willing to trust it and thereby learn to use it, or vice versa. The use of this power develops our faith in it and through constant use our faith increases.

We learn to swim confidently through the water, not fighting it, relaxed and easy, one stroke at a time. But there comes a time when our strength falters and we tire; do we not stop now and then to roll over on our backs and float? This is our time of prayer and meditation, our Eleventh Step. We relax into this power greater than ourselves and thereby gain renewed strength and understanding.

We cannot swim nor float well if we are tense and fearful. The more we relax and accept, the more buoyant we become. We learn that fear is lack of faith and by using the Third Step we learn to let go of everything we do want and of everything we don't want, to "let go and let God," and our faith increases as we learn to pray.

After a day of teaching I used to leave the shore with never a thought of applying these principles to my everyday life. Now through AA I'm learning to try to live as the Twelfth Step suggests, applying these principles to every moment of my life to the best of my ability, living one day at a time. The rewards in contentment, peace of mind, health and happiness have been beyond my wildest expectations.

And I'm sober today, which is all that matters and for which I'm deeply grateful.

J. J.
Buffalo, New York

Back In the Saddle Again
February 1989

Winter morning: air like glass, clear and cold and fragile. I seem to float across the earth, resting on my saddle. For the moment I have the park to myself; there is only one solitary runner on the trail ahead. I know I will overtake him on the straightaway, but he will pass me going uphill. The age-old contest between human and bicycle. I bleat my horn and put on a burst of speed. I can hear him panting as I pass.

There are moments when I wonder how I got here. This is not where I would have expected, 10 years ago or even five, to be today. A better guess would have been jail or a hospital.

I reach the bottom of the incline and begin pumping painfully upward. Usually there are other bikes passing me easily, but today I'm alone on the trail and fear no embarrassment. It was only a week ago that I discovered I could now pedal all the way to the top of this hill without stopping. I begin breathing with my mouth open, sweat in my eyes. I am always amazed at younger people who can carry on a normal conversation while climbing this grade.

Sometimes the conversations I overhear are hilarious. A young couple passes me traveling in the other direction at 20 miles per hour. The woman berates her boyfriend: "Suddenly you start talking about chicken sandwiches! I can't believe you!" (Now what was that about, I wonder.)

By the time I reach the top of the hill my thigh muscles are beyond agony. Yet once again it all becomes worthwhile—the summit, the long downgrade stretching out ahead. Without stopping, I plunge over.

The earth gathers speed and flashes past. There's no sound but the wind in my face. Sometimes I imagine I'm a bird, coasting down the air. A bicycle is simple and elegant, like a bird. Riding like this is a form of meditation; I think of it as a part of my Eleventh Step.

There are three secret rules for riding a bicycle, which you won't find in any bike books. They are:

Easy does it.

One day at a time.

Keep coming back.

Gliding over the earth like this, I realize suddenly how it was that those bicycle mechanics, the Wright brothers, were inspired to flight. Another hill: My muscles must work again. Yet even climbing is like another aspect of flight—as the eagle or crow churns his way to the top of the sky before he can relax and soar.

I have not owned this machine for long. I remember the Sunday morning I stood on a hillside watching a lone biker coast and thinking, I'm going to get a bicycle! My next thought was, Now, why haven't I ever bought one before this? I've wanted a bicycle for as long as I can remember.

Of course the answer to my question came at once: Fool. You stopped smoking one year ago this month. It would have been stupid to own a bicycle when you were smoking three packs a day. And why did it take you so long to stop smoking? Because it's only been some three years since you quit drinking. Before that, you devoted more than 20 years of your life to the intense and devoted pursuit of imbibing. That's why you have never owned a bicycle. But now you can! (I didn't get sober as soon as I should have. But I got sober as soon as I could.)

An idea occurs to me: I will write an article for Grapevine about my bicycle. I'll call it something like "From Barstool to Bike Saddle." Nah. Who would care about that?

Top of the hill—a short level stretch. I notice in the eastern sky a red-tailed hawk suddenly swoop and dive. I identify. The hawk carried out God's will; its power to climb the sky comes only from him. Where did I get the power to come off my last drunk and climb this hill? Not from me. The only difference is, the hawk doesn't need to pray. He already knows. ("OK, God. Just get me up this last 50 feet. Please.")

Finally, the grand finale of my ride this morning: over the crest of this last hill, a death-defying plummet straight down (well, almost) some 400 feet, then a gentle coast back to where I started.

That final drop is like the diving hawk—the rush of wind and whir of spokes. I must hit 35 miles per hour; it takes only seconds to reach bottom. At last I have truly turned over my life and my will. I plummet so fast I doubt I could stop if I wanted to. Do I experience fear? No, just stark terror. And yet, somehow, I return safely once again to earth.

There was a time, not long past, when the phrase "going downhill fast" would have held an entirely different meaning.

When I get back to my apartment, I am feeling exhilarated. "Born in the Saddle," I decide. No, that isn't true. I was born on a barstool. And I got from one to the other through no effort of my own.

The telephone is ringing. It's my friend Carol wanting to know if I'm going to a meeting tonight. "How was your bike ride?" she asks.

"Effortless," I reply.

B.B.
San Francisco, California

Trudging the Road of Happy Destiny
(Excerpt)
Online Exclusive
December 2011

L ike so many other alcoholics that I have heard share over the years, I was certain that there would be no joy in my life without booze. I was 35 years old and literally dying from alcoholism. I was resigned to the fact that my life may as well be over. I joined the glum lot in AA and became one of those miserable members that "just don't drink," not fully understanding the necessity of working the Steps, being part of the Fellowship and being of service.

Sometime during my first 30 days in the program, I was attending a meeting down by the beach where I came across a flyer for the "Sunset Beach Trudgers." Here was a sober backpacking group that went on monthly hikes into the wilderness and had a Saturday night meeting in the woods. I had always enjoyed camping and communing with nature, but my physical condition at that time was terrible and I knew there was no way that I would be able to hike up a mountain carrying a pack in that shape. I put the Trudgers out of my mind and continued on my journey for over a year, staying sober one day at a time without having much fun at all.

When my one year anniversary passed I made a decision to stop smoking and get in shape. This was more an attempt to find a girl-friend than anything else, but my motives never were in the right place. One Wednesday night at my regular meeting, a man whom I had never seen before came in and announced that there was a great group of alcoholics that went on backpacking trips once a month. He gave me a flyer and it was the same one I had seen when I was newly sober. This time I was ready!

I made some phone calls, borrowed some camping gear and went on my first hike in September 1993. It was the annual trip to Mt. San Jacinto where they take the Palm Springs tram up the mountain and then hiked for two more miles to the campsite. About halfway up the trail I realized that I wasn't as athletic as I thought. I was tired and scared and thought maybe this wasn't such a great idea after all. I stopped to rest for a minute and take a drink of water when it happened.

I took a few deep breaths and surveyed my surroundings. There was a meadow in the not so far off distance and I noticed that there was a deer checking me out. It was as if God hit me over the head with a two-by-four. I was in his backyard and it was breathtaking. I guess what I felt at that moment was the closest thing I had ever known to a spiritual awakening. My fear was gone. I got a second wind and continued up the trail where I found the group of sober alcoholics that would soon become some of my best friends.

Dennis D.
La Palma, California

A Serene Place at 5:00 A.M.
September 1980

B y the age of 45, people are considered to be in their middle years. Sober in AA for six years, I was beginning to feel middle-aged, even though people told me I looked younger.

Mentally, I had grown, I thought. Through the help of the Steps and a therapist, I had been able to get in better contact with my feelings and character defects. Spiritually and physically however, I seemed to be stagnant. My energy felt depleted, and conscious contact with a Higher Power was lacking. I was trying to work the Eleventh Step, but found I was becoming frustrated.

Friends of mine in the program had told me of the benefits they received from the now popular sport of jogging. Being a stubborn sort of alcoholic, I said to myself that it was fine for them but didn't appeal to me. Besides, I have a heavy work load in the spring and summer and couldn't possibly fit jogging into my life.

But I took an inventory of my physical self in the past, and I recalled that I was physically, mentally and spiritually healthier when my body was active.

So one day in May, from out of the blue I got the desire to start jogging. I am a golf course superintendent, and I maintain over 100 acres of green grass where I can run to my heart's content, with nobody to see me and laugh but the birds and squirrels.

I started my new sport with an eagerness and determination I hadn't possessed in years. The first day was exciting, to say the least. It was raining, with thunder and lightning to add a little spice to my journey. I thought I would drop after the first 100 yards, but I got a second wind and kept going. I guess I jogged about a mile, and I couldn't believe the joy I experienced in this accomplishment. Gratitude began to fill my heart and soul. I just knew my Higher Power got me through that mile, because I was very much out of shape.

After a week, my eyes opened to the fact that this was indeed my Higher Power showing me what his will was for me. He not only wanted me to stay away from a drink a day at a time, but also wanted me to improve my mind and body so I could enjoy my sobriety to the fullest. For me, this is the Eleventh Step in action. Jogging has become a daily routine for me now. My mind is alert to many things, especially the presence of God. Each workout is concluded with prayer and meditation.

It hasn't been easy, but in my experience, nothing worthwhile is. A golf course is a very serene place at 5:00 A.M. I appreciate the fruits of my labor today. And oh yes, the grass does seem a lot greener.

B. F.
Connecticut

Sink or Swim
Online Exclusive
December 2016

I got to the rooms of AA with huge reservations. Really, the only working knowledge I had of Alcoholics Anonymous was that alcoholics could never drink again, and I was not convinced that was what I wanted. I did want the consequences of my drinking to stop—the mini nervous breakdowns, the insomnia, the incredible loss of time (during the long winters in Indiana, there were times when I was uncertain if it was day or night), and the inconsolable crying jags.

Even so, actually quitting the drink was not terribly appealing. My alcoholic tendencies have been around for much of my adult life. Although I experimented with alcohol early in my teen years, I was a high school and college athlete and focused on those commitments. Being an extremely physically active teen, I sought out physical activity after I graduated from college and became heavily involved in community softball leagues (some call it "beer league ball" of course!), as well as running competitively in community (and eventually nationwide) racing events (many of those events sponsored by beer distributors).

I didn't quit drinking when I first entered the rooms of AA one January day—it happened to be January 6, the feast of the Epiphany—but let's just say I certainly was drinking very cautiously. I had gotten caught up in a several week spree over the holidays and really didn't know how, or if, I could get out of this one. My partner was fearful I would not be able to return to work after the Christmas break. In early January, after a string of drunken days, I lapsed into a deep sadness and state of irrational fear. My partner never really knew what to do with me or for me when I would get to this place, but she thankfully called a friend who knew addiction and recovery quite well and was active in Al-Anon.

I was strongly discouraged from quitting cold turkey without medical help or a regressive weaning process from the booze, and a sick sense of relief fell over me: Thank God I can still drink! In my early days of contemplating acceptance of this disease as my own, I was a trembling, nauseous mess. I found myself religiously attending meetings, listening intently, reading voraciously—yet slowly but surely drinking more and more. With the help of my disease, I threw caution to the wind after two months of AA fellowship. I woke early on a Saturday morning in spring with full intentions of a daylong investment in home repair and cleaning. I headed out to grab a few groceries a little after sunrise and in less than 15 minutes I found myself mixing a drink in a gas station coffee cup.

I found myself fighting the drink fiercely that day, dumping it in the sink one minute and heading back to the liquor mart the next. I know that I wanted to be "done," but alcohol's grip was dictatorial. At last, I was provided overwhelming evidence of my absolute powerlessness. Three shaky days later I finally surrendered, and this time I had no reservations about the gravity of my condition. The morning I finally decided to receive a 24-hour token, I had been sober for 10 days and never felt so relieved in all of my life. I didn't have to live with King Alcohol anymore and I didn't have to do any of this recovery business alone.

My current recovery is grounded in a solid, day-by-day effort of readings, meetings and prayer. I have come across many analogies in my recovery—how some real-life situations mimic the process of working the Steps and working on recovery. My favorite is one I will share with my AA family here. I have been a competitive road runner/ racer most of my adult life and during those years of training (running distance and speed workouts and weight training) quite a bit of focus has been on honing the muscles in my lower body. After experiencing some leg injuries though, I began to seek out other activity. I have never been a strong swimmer, but that activity was easy on my body and provided me with a great sense of challenge, since I was not a very skilled swimmer. I remember getting into the pool for workouts and of course used the only set of muscles that I knew how to effectively engage—my legs. I kicked my way through workout after workout, leaving the pool absolutely exhausted and very disappointed in my lack of ability to complete any swimming distance that would give me a sense of accomplishment.

Frustrated, I sought help from an accomplished swimmer, who was able to point out to me immediately that I was using the wrong set of muscles. If I continued to use my leg muscles as the primary method of moving through my workout, I would certainly continue to be exhausted and disappointed in my progress. He suggested I relax my body in the water and allow the buoyancy of my body to work without excessive movement. Use my upper body (arm strokes) in a fluid, rhythmic movement and only use my legs for a few kicks each length of the pool.

What? Change the way I approach my workout? Use a "new" set of muscles? And yet...it worked! I began to develop my upper body through multiple and consistent swim workouts and now I swim many days each week.

So of course this works perfectly as an analogy for my recovery. When I first got into the program, I wanted badly to accomplish some positive recovery outcomes and so I used my "usual muscles." You know the ones—my self-will, my quick judgment of others' journeys in recovery, my ego-driven search for knowledge. I found myself exhausted most times, trying to control myself and others, questioning others' motives and recovery paths, trying to fit the suggestions to my liking, to my comfort zone.

But during a swim workout, I had the epiphany that I needed to develop a set of the spiritual muscles that many of my friends in the Fellowship were using with great success—they are called prayer and meditation. If I exercise my spiritual muscles daily, keep them strong and ready to respond, chances are that when I am truly in need I can engage them to help me handle any difficulty or challenge I face. I no longer view my recovery path as a difficult, exhausting workout, but instead, with my continued efforts toward spiritual fitness, I am able to step up, show up, and do the right thing. When faced with the choice to sink or swim, I choose to swim!

Kim H.
Muncie, Indiana

Two Wheel Contact
November 2012

After a healthy breakfast my favorite Eleventh Step tool is a bicycle and a half-hour ride before work. I especially like a stretch along the river behind the high school where I occasionally see deer, hawks, ducks and geese. On rare occasions, like twice last summer, I was blessed with the sighting of a bald eagle, and these were both awesome experiences. I always get to see the start of a new day with the sun coming up as I head east. I try to share the joy of the ride by greeting the runners and walkers I meet. I also try to practice some humility by picking up cans and litter. When I'm really spiritually connected I don't worry about the source of the trash but just accept it and pick it up. I do believe that the bicycle helps me keep closer to my Higher Power. I can think about my daily readings, pray, meditate, feel gratitude and prepare for the coming day.

Thanks AA, for this way of life sure beats the guilt, shame and hangovers from the mornings of my drinking career.

Anonymous
Mason City, Iowa

Sk8ing Through Life
September 2005

It's a perfect summer Saturday afternoon in midtown Sacramento. The yearning to commune with my skateboard and to get back to what used to be everything to me is pulling me to the converted warehouse that is the closest skate sanctuary from my room at the halfway house on 23rd to the end of B Street on the other side of the railroad tracks down by the American River. Absentmindedly, I readjust the chinstrap on my helmet as I skate along, thinking about the tricks I'm going to try.

The early afternoon light flickers in high through the broad leaves overhead and the wind cools the beading sweat on the back of my neck as I near the railroad tracks. The hairs on my arm stand on end as I realize I'm already putting expectations on my session just by imagining what I want to see happen. I really hate that word, expectations. Alcoholics Anonymous—of which I'm a six month and still counting member—suggests living without them because expectations screw everything up: relationships, sessions, lives, and even perfect summer afternoons in Sac town.

Hmmm. I don't want to ruin my session before I even get there, so I have to let those expectations go. Have to turn 'em over to the Big Kahuna in the sky. Just need to let it flow, have fun, kick back, and watch, because more will always be revealed.

When I arrive at the end of the roughshod road and step into the cavernous yawn of the old warehouse that is the skate cathedral, I am in awe. A ramp has miraculously appeared since my last visit. Six feet tall, 24 feet wide, seven-foot extensions and steel coping make the ramp a tantalizing temptation. I check my helmet strap and jump on. The motion generates a sound something akin to a giant vacuum cleaner on slo-mo. Vhroomm! Vhrooom! with each pass it goes.

Coming off a 50/50, I lose my footing and slam my head against the masonite ramp. Lying on the flat bottom, my head rings as little sparks of light flicker in my peripheral vision like an acid flashback.

I run back up the steep eight-foot transition, drop in, and try again as I shake off the shock of the first slam. I slowly build up speed and then, arming myself with all the self-will I can muster, I drop in, pop off the lip, grab the outside edge of my board, and hold on for dear life. For too long, I hold on. I hold on even though it doesn't feel right. Paying for my willfulness and ignorance of my intuition, I slam hard again. My head is ringing. Stars are flying. My elbows are screaming again in bruised and swollen pain.

This is insane, I think, while painfully righting myself from the prone position of the slam. I need to step back and reevaluate my approach because my way just isn't working.

My will got me into AA so why should I try and impose it here? Wallowing in self-pity and watching the other skaters enjoy their session, the definition of insanity that is thrown around the rooms of AA comes to mind. They say insanity is doing the same thing over and over again expecting different results. I figure that I need to do something different.

The late afternoon light and the delta breeze waft serenely over us and through the park. I'm looking down at the mammoth "U" structure before me. A prayer just might release me from the bondage of fear and of self. This notion, as if by providence, pops into my head. Remembering all those foxhole prayers made during my drunken years of debauchery and self-indulgence causes doubts. This prayer has to be different. Asking God to help me land this trick would be just like all those selfish 911 prayers I had made when I was out there. I sit for a minute, enjoying the breeze while thinking about thinking.

What is my part in this whole affair of self-will run riot? How has fear come to run my thoughts? Rather than trying to do the Big Kahuna's will, I'm trying to impose my own, I realize. It has to be his will, not mine. If I can't pray for what I have, I have to pray for the Big K in the sky to remove my fear. Accepting that it is there is the first step to liberation. Of course! The Serenity Prayer! How could I be so oblivious? Closing my eyes, I say it out loud.

"Oh, Big Kahuna in the sky, grant me the serenity to accept the things I cannot change, the courage to change the things I can, and wisdom to know the difference."

Opening my eyes, I see another skater on the opposite deck of the ramp smiling at me. I smile back.

Breathe, relax, trust the process, I say to myself, envisioning the set up for the air before even dropping into the transitions. I have to place the front foot just behind the front truck bolts, position the back foot to pop the tail off the lip, have a good amount of speed, ready the left hand to grasp the outside edge of my board while in the air for a split second, and then let go. It's the last step, releasing the board in mid air, that takes faith. If I do the proper footwork, the aforementioned steps—just as I do in Alcoholics Anonymous with the Twelve Steps of recovery—and have enough velocity, all it would take to pull myself back into the ramp would be the belief, the faith, that it was possible. I have to let go of it completely and trust the process, just as I do in AA.

Instinct and logic tell me to bail out of it when I hit my peak in the air. They scream at me, "You can't just fly through the air like that! What about gravity, huh?" It's counter-intuitive and goes against all logic, that's how I know that it is spiritually the right thing to do. If all I have is a dollar in my pocket and I'm at a meeting, logic tells me to save it for myself for later. If I give it to AA, and have faith in the process, it will come back to me in ways I can't even imagine.

Spirituality is not based on logic, it is faith-driven. Faith makes the impossible possible. Faith has allowed me to be clean and sober for six months. Flying through the air on my skateboard is a test of faith that releases me from the bondage of self, helps me confront my fear, and takes me away from my overly analytical, logical mind.

One more deep breath before I drop in. Vhroomm! Vhroomm! Rolling backward into a tail stall on the opposing wall, I position my feet. Dropping back in, I build speed by crouching low. I'm popping the tail off the lip now, up and over the coping I fly. Grabbing the outside edge of my board, I hit my peak. Now is the moment of truth. I've done all I can at this point. I have to let go and trust in the process: courage instead of fear. Momentarily, I float. Then, the most beautiful sound in the world: all four wheels of my skate touching down on the ramp's smooth surface at the same time. It's a sound of self-assuredness, so satisfying, clean and true. I'm rolling up the other wall of the ramp now, smiling.

Afterward, the other skater asks me, "Were you praying before you dropped in?"

"Yep. I was," I answer. "It makes me remember why I started skating."

"Cool."

Baxter J.
Sacramento, California

The Serenity Prayer

Using a beloved prayer to connect and pray

A ny craftsperson can explain that to do a job properly requires using the proper tools. For many alcoholics in AA, stretching back over decades, the tool often reached for to restore emotional balance has been the Serenity Prayer. "The more I say it, read it, hear it—the more profoundly I feel its effectiveness," writes L.T. in the opening story of this chapter, "These Twenty-Five Words."

The simple grace and pared down logic of this prayer have been helping alcoholics sort through the challenges of daily living since AA's cofounder Bill W. and the early AA pioneers first came across it in a newspaper obituary notice. "Never had we seen so much AA in so few words," wrote Bill in the book *AA Comes of Age*. Often attributed to Rev. Reinhold Niebuhr of the Union Theological Seminary, Bill noted, "We count its writer among our great benefactors."

AAs have come to use the prayer in many different ways—both direct and indirect. Carl B. in the story "OK With Me," thought of it as counting to 10—"Slowing down my brain and mouth before the anger built up or the depression sucked me down"—a kind of safety valve bringing his emotional temperature down. Writer B.C. in the article "An Answer Without a Prayer," experienced the power of the Serenity Prayer more indirectly just by saying it together with others at the end of AA meetings, no matter how reluctantly. "I came to believe," the author writes, "that their belief was more powerful than my unbelief. That experience became the threshold to the Second and Third Steps for me, and my sobriety and serenity have continued to improve steadily since that time."

These Twenty-Five Words
April 1979

The Serenity Prayer has always played an important role in my recovery process, but only lately have I recognized the true value within these 25 words. The more I say it, read it, hear it—the more profoundly I feel its effectiveness as it relates to the handling of my one-day-at-a-time living experiences.

If I refuse to accept what I am powerless to change, I am negating the opportunity that God gives me to do so. He always grants me the serenity that goes hand in hand with the acceptance of that which I am incapable of changing. However, the key question I must ask myself is: Am I willing to accept this serenity that he so graciously offers me? I must remind myself of this whenever I think I have accepted something and then discover that my serenity is nil.

If I am sincerely trying to live according to the guidance of our AA principles, I will recognize that I have chosen not to accept the unchangeable, but only to tolerate it. To merely tolerate a situation or a person's shortcomings is to settle for a half measure. And there is the reason for my serenity deficit.

As for the second part of the prayer, "courage to change" certain circumstances comes from inner strength—my abundant source of supply that my Higher Power constantly nourishes. But I must choose to draw upon this strength. It is always there—I need only be willing to use it.

The third part, "wisdom to know the difference," is the divine key to acceptance and courage. For me, this wisdom is revealed through the practice of our Eleventh Step, "Sought through prayer and meditation to improve our conscious contact with God *as we understood Him,* praying only for knowledge of His will for us and the power to carry that out."

Because this is an honest program, I must admit that I fall short many times in applying this interpretation of the Serenity Prayer. I realize I am still growing emotionally and spiritually. After several years of sobriety through the grace of God and AA, I am only beginning to acknowledge the God-power within me.

But by simply expressing my personal concept of this traditional and meaningful prayer, I am enabled to view with more clarity where I am today and where I was yesterday. Tomorrow is yet to be, but should God grant me another day, then hope, courage and strength, through the implementation of the Twelve Steps and the Serenity Prayer, will be sufficiently provided to meet my every need. This I believe.

L. T.
St. Petersburg, Florida

Hula Hoop Larry and the Serenity Prayer
Online Exclusive
January 2020

I t's amusing and endearing to me that we do not get hung up about knowing someone's last name in our program, but we do often use descriptors to tell the Bobs, Bills and Daves apart.

The Serenity Prayer has haunted me for almost 60 years. It hung in my aunt's house and was cause for silent frustration to me as a 10-year-old. I read it and thought to myself: God grant me the serenity to accept the things I cannot change, courage to change the things I can, and wisdom to know the difference. This is a riddle—who's gonna explain how to tell the difference between these two ideas anyway? Of course, I never had the courage to ask anyone about it.

Anyway, I was at a roundup recently where I met my third Larry. Over the weekend, he shared about a hula hoop and it provided some much-needed clarity for me. I asked him if he was OK with me calling him "Hula Hoop Larry" since I didn't know his last name. He assured me this was OK.

Our topic during the meeting was serenity and the Serenity Prayer. Many shared that this was more elusive than accessible, to which I could relate. Some discussed prayer, meditation, daily readings and so on. Larry talked about how his serenity was directly proportional to taking care of himself. He described his boundary as being about as big as a hula hoop if he were standing in the middle of its circle. He said, "All the territory inside the hula hoop is my concern, my business and within my power to change; everything outside of it is none of my business, and out of my control."

That makes it so easy for me to visualize how to understand the difference between:

- the things I cannot change (outside hula hoop)

- the things I can change (my thoughts, feelings, beliefs and actions inside the hula hoop) and

- the wisdom to know the difference (the hula hoop and the connection to a Higher Power)

My sponsor says that taking care of ourselves is a full time job, one we are maybe doing for the first time in our lives. Today I know that I am responsible for keeping that connection to my Higher Power real, consistent and possible. I'm the one who walks away when the connection gets broken. Because of this connection I can learn to choose to love myself, do the next right thing, to see the best in people and to accept life on life's terms. All within a little circle of red hula hoop plastic (mine would be red, of course).

This proves to me beyond the shadow of a doubt that I am a visual learner. I recently heard that Hula Hoop Larry has passed on, to be with his wife Joan. Thank goodness for hula hoops and for the gifts that come from people like Larry, sharing their wisdom in meetings. Thank you all for my sobriety.

Becky P.

Attitude Adjustment
November 1997

" **A**nd let's always remember that meditation is in reality intensely practical." —*Twelve Steps and Twelve Traditions*

If I'd been instructed to pray and meditate, and then to wait around for however long it took to see some results, it's not likely I'd still be doing it. That's not me. I'm not results-oriented necessarily, just untrusting, impatient and scornful of magical thinking. I need to see some immediate connection between my actions and their results, even though, in 12 years of sobriety, I've come to accept that the results are mostly out of my hands.

So the claim that meditation and prayer are intensely practical caught my attention in the beginning. I became willing to try something I didn't understand or believe in for the intensely practical reason that, on my own, I couldn't stop drinking. My sponsor insisted that prayer and meditation could enlist a power greater than myself in my efforts.

I tried it, didn't understand it, didn't believe in it. And it worked anyway: I stopped drinking. I wasn't the only one in my life who noticed this practical result. My immediate family—with whom I share a good deal of intellectual arrogance and emotional insecurity—were relieved to see me sober, but equally skeptical that my "religious conversion" would last any longer than the few months I'd previously devoted to any of a dozen other passing fancies.

Twelve years later my arrogant family is still skeptical, but trusting that this prayer business keeps me out of trouble. And I believe in prayer, but still don't understand it. I've seen enough intensely practical results to give the devil himself pause to reconsider his convictions. Yet I still forget. This practice makes extraordinary things happen in my life that, when I'm not paying attention, appear ordinary. Precisely because they are practical, the results of my prayers are often easy to miss or misinterpret. So I need reminding.

Yesterday at work, for instance. A small task I performed (outside the purview of my job) corrected a mistake my supervisor had made. Instead of thanks, my effort received a written reprimand for stepping out of bounds. After thinking over the situation, I apologized for not consulting said supervisor first, admitting where I'd been wrong, but secretly expecting thanks in return for saving this person some trouble. None was forthcoming. I was warned not to cross the boundary again. Fellow employees smirked, knowing that the new guy—Mr. Sure-I'll-Do-That—had had his hand slapped.

Something I've learned from my inventories is that given a resentment to work on, my mind has a life of its own. This one set the mental gears churning. I knew two things would work to turn off the mental noise: First, saying out loud to another sober alcoholic all the crazy things my mind was working over; second, out-shouting the mental grumbling with prayer. The latter seemed a practical solution under the circumstances. I went back to work, with the Serenity Prayer and my resentment toward my supervisor cranking at equal volume on my brain.

I wasn't paying attention to the content of the Serenity Prayer, just repeating it for the comfort of its sound. But in retrospect I see that fancy diction aside, it is an unqualified and uncompromising demand. There is not humble consideration for "if it be Thy will," or "in Thine own time" in this prayer. One might just as well say, "Hey Big Guy! How about some serenity, courage, and wisdom so I can make a few changes down here? And I don't mean tomorrow."

In this light, I understand better why I took to the prayer right from the beginning of my sobriety. I also understand why my Higher Power keeps a special place in his heart for alcoholics—the same way I do for little children and wild animals.

Back on the job about two hours later, still grumbling and mumbling, I rounded a corner of my workplace and nearly walked into a man I knew from AA but hadn't seen for three years. In the few minutes we both could spare from work, we caught each other up on recent events. I heard myself telling him about some extraordinarily fortunate things that have happened in my life these past few years. And I didn't fail to notice that when I went back to work, I felt much better and the cement mixer in my mind had ground to a halt.

I went directly from work to my weekly Step study group where we were reading Step Eleven. When we came upon the passage about meditation and prayer being intensely practical, the recognition struck that I'd been too busy to notice.

I'd been disturbed by what I considered to be the unfairness of life. I'd said the Serenity Prayer over and over—in essence a direct request to God to grant me serenity, courage and wisdom. As in all my experience, God didn't reach down and inject me with what I thought I needed. Instead I was given an opportunity to take some action. Without realizing what I was doing, I recounted a substantial and growing gratitude list to an old acquaintance from the Fellowship. I noticed that I felt better afterward. I probably worked better too.

I've seen quicker and more dramatic results with some of my prayers, never for material things, but frequently for the spirit and attitude I need to stay in touch with life's abundance and opportunity. This I've found to be intensely practical. With an open mind and loving heart I never fail to see that I've been provided more than enough for a life of meaning, dignity, freedom, usefulness and hope. Practically speaking, it's a life second to none.

Anonymous
York Harbor, Maine

Sounds of Silence
April 2004

My home group usually seizes up if there's a whole 45 seconds of silence between shares. Then someone leaps into the breach, saying, "I'll talk because I just can't stand the silence." This might be part of my problem with meditation. As an alcoholic, I'm used to having a few plates spinning in the air and lots of cunning plans chattering away in my brainpan. The prospect of any kind of silence is truly frightening.

Approaching silence is what we do when we meditate. In prayer, as I have been taught to think of it, I get to yak to the Higher Power and, God knows, I'm comfortable with that. But listening? Not my forté.

We are encouraged in the Big Book to look for our own methods in this area. That scares me too, because when I'm not busy resisting everything and everyone, I want to be completely dictated to.

Early in my sobriety, my first sponsee told me that she had no clue at all about meditation, and sitting still just made her "committee" get louder. Miraculously, when I opened my mouth to answer her, someone else talked. That someone quoted an oldtimer who advised that we let go of our old ideas about what meditation is and try to find some place that already exists in our lives where we feel the bondage of self drop away. My sponsee knew exactly what that meant and told me that when she went to swim laps at the pool, there was a point when it was just the water and the movement and the sound. "That's it! Go there," I said. She said "But that's exercise, not meditation."

Yes, it is meditation. A little research showed me that, historically, people have tried to reach that state she described in her swimming many, many ways, and not a few of them have involved movement. In fact, AA cofounder Bill W. practiced a walking and breathing meditation to get through his depression while he was writing *Twelve Steps and Twelve Traditions.*

Years later, another sponsee told me she couldn't meditate because she couldn't stop her mind. But the point of meditation is not to stop the mind, but to watch the mind—to develop a witness position on that running commentary of self-obsessed fear that can dominate. I believe anything that helps me do that is meditation.

Another suggestion that has helped me is to say the Serenity Prayer one word at a time, a full breath in between each word. This begins to work wonders with the first word and the first breath: "God, aaaaah...." It works because it turns me in the direction of the program instead of the direction of my self-obsessed thoughts. Meditation is a change of mental direction, nothing more complicated than that. I understand changing mental direction; I used to use gin to change my mental direction all the time. Now I have these easier and more effective ways.

Like needing the "right" pen to write the Fourth Step, some of us procrastinate about meditating because we can't find the "right" time of day or the "right" place. There is no wrong place or time for "God, aaaaah...." and it only takes a couple of seconds. It improves my direction even if I get interrupted after the first word. This corresponds with the direction Bill gives at the end of Step Three in the "Twelve and Twelve": "In all times of emotional disturbance or indecision, we can pause, ask for quiet, and in the stillness say: 'God, grant me the serenity....'"

The key word there for the willingness to change mental direction is "pause."

Jean C.
Eugene, Oregon

Dear HP
November 2014

When I walked in the doors of AA, I heard a lot of talk about praying. People told me to get on my knees in the morning and at night and say the Third Step Prayer, the Seventh Step Prayer, the Lord's Prayer and the Serenity Prayer. They told me to pray about this and that and to put them in my prayers, adding that they would put me in theirs. And of course, people told me to pray for those I resented or disliked.

I heard all this talk about prayer with very little working knowledge. The only prayer I did say was Grace, before dinner. But I'd also scream and curse at God because I blamed him for all my problems. And let's not forget all the wet and dry drunk rants and raves that I yelled out to the trees, chairs or any object in my path. I was filled with fear, anger and frustration that life was not on my terms. But I could no longer drink or scream these feelings away.

I had a shaky start with a new Higher Power and with Step Two. I had to discard my old punishing fire-and-brimstone Higher Power. I had to replace it with a loving and tolerant one. I still didn't believe my new HP cared about me. So I was told just to "believe that I believed."

When I moved on to Step Three, it was time to hit my knees. There I was, on my knees and elbows on the bed saying the Third Step prayer. It really felt weird for about a month. It was just words at first, but I kept saying the prayer until it didn't feel weird any more. And when I was upset or wanted a drink, I would repeat the Serenity Prayer over and over, sometimes out loud and sometimes just in my mind. Somehow it seemed to help.

When I felt on shaky ground, I'd ask my HP for help to get me to meetings. I'd ask for help when I thought the world would fall in on me. I was starting to believe my new HP did love and care for me. Then in walked Step Five; I never saw it coming. When it came time to tell God my Fourth Step I didn't know what was going on in my head. I thought God knew everything, so I didn't have to tell him. Then someone pointed out why telling God my Fourth Step shouldn't be a big deal. Man, that caught me in a lie to myself. Well, I did that part of the Fifth Step, for which I'm so grateful. At first I thought my new HP would leave me when I told him what I had done, but I was wrong. Praying to my HP for forgiveness was the most personal thing I've ever done.

I must have said the Serenity Prayer about a million times before I realized that it was telling me how to deal with life's problems (I'm a little slow.) What part of the problem or situation did I need to accept? And what parts did I need to change? The only part I can change is my actions, so I needed to pray for the courage to change them. I also prayed for help accepting other people, places and things. The wisdom part comes with time. Time also taught me to look at the other prayers for guidance—and I have. Wow! What wisdom I found in the prayers. They're guidelines to help me to accept life on life's terms.

I had five years sober when I went back to school and worked the Steps and all of the program to the best of my ability. Still, I had no good job, no good place to live and no hope. I had hit rock bottom in sobriety. So I sat down and wrote my HP a letter. I opened my soul and heart like never before. As tears hit the paper, I kept writing. I wrote until I was empty—until there was nothing left inside. I got an envelope, addressed it to God and took it to a mailbox. As I put my letter in the mailbox the tears fell from my face, and I let go. After the letter was dropped, my life slowly got better, and my faith and relationship with my HP really grew. I hope to always grow toward my HP and to learn more about prayer every day.

Jeff H.
Sturgeon, Missouri

An Answer Without a Prayer
April 1986

During my drinking days, I lived primarily by the principle expressed in the Herbert Spencer quote at the end of the second appendix to the Big Book on spiritual experience. For this reason I had an intense aversion to "organized religion," with which I equated spirituality, and was more or less convinced that I was an atheist. When I came into AA, the Second and Third Steps seemed an insurmountable obstacle to the rest of the Steps, and I became a "two-stepper."

I was desperate to stay sober however, and through the Fellowship of AA I did just that for two and a half years, constantly plagued by the desire to drink. For all of that time the advertisers of alcoholic beverages were hated names simply because I wanted to sample their products again.

Then one day at a family reunion of some two dozen of my relatives, I suddenly became aware that all the people in the room, with the exception of myself, were holding drinks and sipping at them. I discovered I no longer wanted a drink and had not, in fact, even given it a thought. When this realization of the loss of compulsion dawned on me I could hardly wait, like a typical alcoholic, to put it to the test.

That evening, when I was alone again, I examined as many television commercials and magazine liquor ads as I could to see what their effect on me would be. To my amazement there was no effect, except a vast relief that the compulsion was really gone! It was some kind of miracle for me, for I knew I had done nothing to rid myself of that compulsion.

I still could not pray, not even for a return to sanity. How could this have happened then? I hadn't asked any "Higher Power" to help me. The nearest I had come to praying was to repeat the Serenity Prayer with others at meetings. Could this be it? Could this single prayer, repeated at meeting after meeting without conviction on my part, have done it? This had to be the answer. Others at those meetings were not as reluctant as I; perhaps their simple sincerity lent some validity to my repeating the prayer with them.

This is what I came to believe: that their belief was more powerful than my unbelief. That experience became the threshold to the Second and Third Steps for me, and my sobriety and serenity have continued to improve steadily since that time.

I have had the joy of other spiritual experiences since then, but none with greater significance for me. Now, at a moment's thought, God is with me when I need him. It was difficult to learn to pray, but in time pages 63 and 561 of the Big Book and page 101 of *Twelve Steps and Twelve Traditions* showed me the answers. I now converse regularly with my Higher Power, this loving God of my reluctant understanding. He is my friend and companion, and while his response to my prayers may not always be what I expect, he always responds.

He will, I believe, do this for anyone who asks, even if they are not sure they really mean it or even know exactly what they are doing. He will always hear their plea and sooner or later respond, when it is best for them. But we must be patient, you know, for he has so many to love and care for.

B. C.
Revelstoke, British Columbia

OK With Me
August 2006

When I joined AA, I was definitely an agnostic. The whole God thing didn't have anything to do with staying sober, anyway. And in my mind, sobriety was all I needed to get my life back in order.

It didn't matter if you called it a power greater than me, Higher Power, Allah, God, or whatever, it still seemed spacey to me. I mean, come on. Speaking into thin air—or in my head—to something I couldn't see, feel or hear, and then acting as if it would affect my real life here on Earth was just plumb crazy. I needed something a bit more nuts and bolts.

I didn't drink for about three months, got a job, and reentered the everyday world. To my surprise, I felt angry or depressed most of the time. I was howling, ranting, out of control, or I was down in the dumps, useless, pathetic and pitiful. Take your pick.

I saved my feelings for my fellow AAs. I was constantly upset, and it was always someone else's fault. Since I couldn't drink, I made my case at AA meetings.

Tired of my attitude and constant whining, someone suggested I say the Serenity Prayer whenever I felt this way. I might see how powerless I was over the thing I fought against, the person said.

That's great advice, I thought, except I don't believe in your God stuff. "God" is the very first word in that Serenity Prayer thing. But despite my sarcasm, I decided to try saying it without addressing God.

Each time I felt my emotions veer off in either direction, I ran through the mantra. I chose to call it "mantra" because prayer was directed to God. "Mantra" seemed less religious, and maybe a tiny bit spiritual. I thought of it as counting to 10. Slowing down my brain and mouth before the anger built up, or the depression sucked me down. My thoughts and reactions became slower, more measured, and there were fewer drastic mood swings.

I broke my serenity mantra into three separate parts and thought about what each part had to do with any particular situation: acceptance, courage, and choosing action or inaction. The Big Book says it well: "As we go through the day we pause, when agitated or doubtful, and ask for the right thought or action. We constantly remind ourselves we are no longer running the show, humbly saying to ourselves many times each day 'Thy will be done.'"

"Thy" could be anything, right? My will—my thinking—hadn't been very good for a while. In fact, some AA members said my best thinking got me here. I acted out on my thoughts immediately, which always seemed to lead to more trouble in some aspect of my life, and those aspects were my "lives" as brother, son, employee, etc.

Any substitute for my will being done was probably a good thing. I added this on to my mantra. Use whatever works, they said.

How I felt about a situation was really important, usually more important than the situation itself.

"Let it be as it will be," a saying that combined a Buddhist saying and the old Beatles song, popped into my mind one day. That's about as accepting as it gets.

What if the situation was actually wrong, and I couldn't accept it happily, or positively change it? "Accept" didn't mean "like." Just don't become "sore" or "burned up," as the Big Book says about resentments on page 65. How about "And me be OK with it"? Cool. I added these on, too.

How powerless something bothering me really was, I realized, was more important than how powerless I was over it. The need to control, or be helpless, was fading away. I might not have a lot of control over things in my life, but many of those things shouldn't have control over me either. Life wasn't out to get me, anymore than it was there to serve me. It just was.

That's how I developed my version of the Serenity Prayer, which has worked well for me since 1995.

"God, grant me the serenity to accept things I cannot change. courage to change things I can, and the wisdom to discern the difference. Thy will, not mine, be done. Let it be as it will be. And me be OK with it."

Did I say "discern"? Another problem word for me was "know." By now, knowing much of anything, let alone a Higher Power's plan, was beyond me. That's why I asked for help.

"Know" was too arrogant for me, so I looked for a substitute with more humility. The Oxford Dictionary defines "discern" as "to see clearly with the mind and senses." Much better.

I hope you noticed that I got over the "God" word during this process. Most of my hang-ups were nothing more than misunderstandings of the English language, and how I reacted to them.

The Big Book says we'll know we've been restored to sanity when "we have ceased fighting anything or anyone—even alcohol," meaning, when I can be OK with the world the way it is today. My prayer helps me be OK most of the time, and OK is great compared to what I was before. In fact, OK might be the closest and simplest description of serenity I'll ever find. And that's OK with me.

Carl B.
Evansville, Indiana

CHAPTER FIVE

Stars, Mountains, Water and Furry Creatures

Finding a spiritual connection through nature and the universe

---

Trees, the night sky, dogs, cats, birds, a fox—even a rattle-snake. These are the channels to spirituality for some of the writers in this chapter. Without any external criteria defining "Higher Power," each AA member is free to find whatever works best on an individual basis, and nature often provides the means for such discovery.

For Paolina A., in her story "Rock Bottom," throwing rocks into the ocean offered the means of releasing years of self-hatred and character defects. "I recite the Seventh Step Prayer," she writes. "I pick up a rock and throw it in the ocean." Each rock represents a different character defect and having gone through the pile of rocks at her feet she feels lighter, not so alone. "Have I just made conscious contact with my Higher Power?" she asks. "The peace and quiet in my head says yes."

Sometimes animals can reach through the alcoholic fog and touch people in ways that others, even family members, cannot. In the article "Higher Power Unleashed," M.N. writes about a family intervention that failed to get him sober, while his relationship with Rosco, part German shepherd, part mutt, led to a spiritual and emotional bottom that paved the way for recovery. "I now have a great dog walking business," the author writes. "Every day, all day long I'm with the dogs, nature and my belief that God is leading me in a healthy direction."

Spending time in nature—a backyard, a forest, a mountain range—can often clear a pathway to spiritual experience and as articulated in Step Eleven, provide an unshakable foundation for life.

A Thousand Wishes
March 2015

W hen I finally entered the rooms of AA in earnest, I read the Steps over and over. Early in recovery, I attended a meeting focused on Step Eleven. Thinking about this Step, where we "sought through prayer and meditation to improve our conscious contact with God," I realized that I understood how to meditate, but I didn't know how to pray. An analyst by nature and by training, my mind was always spinning, dissecting my thoughts and contemplating my actions. I planned my day each morning and took stock each evening. I analyzed and over-analyzed each and every event of the day, trying to put things into perspective, to grasp the meaning of life, and to understand my role in the universe. But I did not pray.

I've had more religious training than most, with years of formal religious studies from kindergarten until the age of 16. By rote, I'd learned hundreds of prayers, but knew little of their true meaning or intent. I'd sat through thousands of hours of instruction and services, without taking to heart the words I heard. My family celebrated holidays together. They were an enjoyable tradition and ritual, but in no way spiritual events. I was an agnostic, clinging to the belief of some cosmic force, always dismissive of the idea of one true, paramount religion and always skeptical of any single view of an all-powerful God.

The night I returned from rehab, I walked onto my front porch. It was a beautiful, warm summer evening. The stars were shimmering brightly in the sky. I don't know why, but I looked up and said that childhood rhyme, "Star light, star bright, first star I see tonight; I wish I may, I wish I might, have the wish I wish tonight." Then I had to decide on my one wish for the evening, out of all the many things I needed and wanted. This focused me and forced me to decide, for that night, what was the one most important thing for me. Then I made my wish.

I did the same thing the next night—and the night after. Soon, this became my own personal nightly ritual. After about two weeks, I went onto the porch, but it was a cloudy night and the sky was just a dark gray blanket. Even though I couldn't see the stars, I knew they were still there. This gave me comfort, so I made my wish anyway.

One day, I shared my star story with this kind woman in my home group. Her ever-present smile grew even wider. She leaned over and gave me a big hug. Looking into my eyes, she said, "That's so good." I was happy she liked the story. Then she said, "That means you're praying every day." Wow, how her words struck me. This insight she so simply stated opened the door for me.

Indeed, I had been praying without even realizing it! In some small way, I did have faith in the order of the universe and its permanence, embodied in those stars. I had hope, not that all my wishes would be granted, but that important ones might come to pass. Prayer, faith and hope then made me able to separate religious doctrine from spirituality. Spirituality led me to begin to believe in a Higher Power. That belief helped me begin my journey toward discovering a God of my understanding. By the time I really started working Step Eleven, I knew how to both meditate and pray.

It's now over a thousand wishes from my first one that summer evening. I can't remember them all, but I vividly remember the very first one. On that night, I knew what I most wanted: I wished for sanity. Over time, I have grown to understand that a prerequisite for sanity is sobriety. More recently, my wishes are for more moments of serenity, sanity and sobriety. To me, that's the progression the Steps lead us through.

A wish is a hope for tomorrow. My Higher Power and the AA program are what give me hope today.

Anonymous

Rock Bottom
July 2009

Monday morning: my sponsor has asked me to make a list of my character defects so that we can do Steps Six and Seven when we meet later in the day. It's been weeks since I've met with her to do Step work, and I've been wallowing in my character defects since I finished reading her my Fifth Step. I'm anxious and frustrated. I'm angry about other issues in my life. I'm ready to get some relief and do these two Steps. Unfortunately, our schedules change and we can no longer meet. I can't hang onto these any longer, but I'm not really sure what to do.

Earlier in the week I had practiced talking to God. I definitely can admit to believing in a Higher Power, but I've always questioned whether or not she actually has any interest in me on a personal level. My sponsor has been encouraging me for months to practice praying, even if I don't think it will do anything. She also suggested writing a letter to God, allowing her to respond. It was during that assignment that I found myself having a full-blown conversation with God in my journal. In that dialogue I wrote that all I wanted to do was go throw rocks in the ocean.

So, back to Monday morning: What to do with myself now that we're not meeting? I debate a meeting, and I debate driving to the beach to throw rocks in the ocean. The beach wins. It's a drizzly, gray morning and I'm not really prepared for the weather, but I don't care. I drive to a beach that I know has lots of rocks. I climb down to the sand and sit on the rocks. I have my list of character defects and a marker, and I decide to write my defects on the rocks so I can then throw them in the water. At first I think I'll choose little rocks that are easy to throw. Then I realize my first character defect is "self-hatred" and that definitely warrants a big rock. Most of the rocks I choose are not so little. I sit and write and sit and write, until next to me I have a big pile of rocks.

I realize that the water is quite far from where I'm sitting, and I have a big pile of rocks that I'm not sure how to get there. I take the blanket I'm sitting on and bundle them up in it. I laugh when I go to pick the blanket up and realized how heavy my pile of character defects is! I am so ready to let these go. I walk to the water and empty the blanket on the sand.

I stare at the sky and I stare at the waves and just start talking and crying and asking God to please help me because I'm tired and she has to help me because I'm done trying to do it all myself. After seven-and-a-half months of sobriety, I finally stop holding onto the one last bit of self-will. I finally allow myself to really pray for God's care and protection. I recite the Seventh Step prayer. I pick up a rock and throw it in the ocean. I pick up another rock, say the Seventh Step prayer again and throw it in the ocean. Rock, prayer, toss, rock, prayer, toss. I look down when there are two rocks remaining and laugh. Of course they are the two biggest rocks and my two most stubborn defects. I let those go, too. And then I feel light. And I feel not so alone. And I feel God. Did I just say that? Have I just had a spiritual experience? Have I just made conscious contact with my Higher Power? The peace and quiet in my head says yes.

I walk back to where I had been sitting on the rocks. I've always heard the expression, "nature abhors a vacuum," and I ask God to fill the space that's been emptied with character assets. I ask for willingness, humility, love, honesty and compassion. I thank her for being present, for accepting my character defects. I realize the ocean is the best "God box" ever. I realize I'm no longer as afraid to be alone with my overwhelming feelings because I can just return to the water's edge and pray to God.

Praying is very new for me. I'm not really sure how to do it.

Paolina A.
Venice, California

Under the Ginkgo Tree
February 2011

I'd heard no one's experience on Step Two. I was not reading the Big Book; my sponsor was not taking me through it either, so I was confused. I didn't want to believe in God. I was scared to use the word. I felt uncomfortable for those who did, although I had called out to him once or twice when I was in real danger and I was led to safety.

I would lie in bed wondering about what those church people knew that I didn't, but I was afraid of them, so I wasn't going to approach them and ask. As a child I went to church a number of times with two of my siblings. We stole the tithe our parents gave us, spending it on lollies. Eventually the elders told us to leave, because we laughed too much. We lied and told our parents we didn't want to go back.

Now sober, I visited two different churches, seeking this Higher Power I was meant to have. I didn't find it and I decided church wasn't for me. These visits left me more bemused.

"Find a power greater than you," I kept getting told by AA members. But where do I find it? How do I find it? What the heck is a power greater than me? I was too embarrassed to ask, because I didn't want to appear stupid. I prayed to whatever I had called out previously to for help. I asked that I be shown a power greater than myself.

Days, weeks, months later—I cannot remember—I went into a botanical garden and in my favorite spot by a lake, I lay down under the ginkgo tree. I watched the soft white clouds high up above me as they moved past the full-leafed branches of the tree. A thought came: Gosh, I couldn't stand alive against the seasons the way this tree does. Immediately, it occurred to me that here was a power greater than me. I laughed at this realization—I was happy! I now understood. It didn't occur to me at that moment that my prayer had been answered. I know it to be so today.

For many years in Alcoholics Anonymous I would not share that initially any ginkgo tree was my Higher Power, for fear of being ridiculed or judged. I share it today as a part of my spiritual journey, because, as it says in the Big Book: "Much to our relief, we discovered we did not need to consider another's conception of God."

Jennifer P.
Christchurch, New Zealand

Higher Power Unleashed
November 2016

I was a great star athlete in high school and played sports in college. I was a good teacher and got a master's degree. I was never going to be an alcoholic. Yet, when I was in 7th grade, and my parents were going through a horrible divorce, and my sense of security and belief in a Higher Power crumbled, I started to get drunk to free myself from a horrible depression.

I felt free when I drank. It took away the piercing pain, as my home life was demolished right before my eyes and my parents refused to talk to each other. My dad went on a hunger strike and my mom turned to the bottle more aggressively. I felt like my whole life was a lie because for 12 years my family and parents had always filled me and my two sisters with love and reassurance, and put our family first. Now, out of nowhere, we moved to two separate apartments, and I watched my parents' marriage disintegrate into a battle of hate. So when I got drunk on weekends and cried to my friends and talked about my unhappiness, drinking was my great release. It gave me a weird satisfaction.

I was in the 8th grade when, in a black out, I visited a hospital for the first time. Later, I found out I had made a scene at my best friend's house and screamed at the cops. I had stitches across my head to prove it. I was lucky sports saved me from becoming a full-time alkie, because sports gave me the escape from my troubles that I so longed for.

Again, I could never be an alcoholic, because I didn't drink daily. I was an angry 28-year-old teacher who had accomplished all her work and educational goals, yet I was filled with self-hate. I hated the concept of God, as well as the word God. Over the next four years, I turned into a daily drinker and lost my great teaching job because I left weed in the classroom. In a rage-fueled blackout, I burned down my apartment by leaving candles lit all over the place. Before I passed out, I remember thinking, There's nothing to live for. I woke up in a burning bed. My two amazing cats died from smoke inhalation; I loved my cats more than I loved myself. I couldn't stand to be sober for an hour, so I drank to forget all that I had destroyed. I was finally exactly who I never wanted to be—an alcoholic.

Finally, my family held an intervention and told me they would not be in my life unless I went to AA. Well, I did, sort of. But I did not believe in God. And I would act sober, yet I relapsed secretly every few months. I never believed I would live a sober life. I was spiritually sick.

I developed a best friend named Rosco. He was a beautiful dog (part German shepherd, part mutt) that I walked, and he was always happy to see me. We spent hours in the park, where he would fetch three tennis balls at a time. I began to feel present and alive because of his unconditional love and affection for me.

Then one night, on my last relapse, I went to pick up Rosco. But instead of running around the table with excitement, he put his tail down and walked away—our spirits were no longer aligned. I was not present, I smelled like booze and Rosco wanted nothing to do with me. My heart hurt. I had my first spiritual and emotional bottom. I drank one more time after that and, on February 8th, I hope to celebrate seven years of sobriety.

I continued to walk Rosco and play with him in the snow for hours, because his spirit and zest for life was infectious. He made me feel happy in my own skin; he showed me the beauty in life—just as it is. Then one night, while we were lying in the snow and he had his lovable head resting on my shoulder, I looked up at the sky and every cell in my body came alive. With every fiber of my being, I was happy to be alive. I felt the presence of God. I felt a deep love and friendship. The beautiful fresh snow and the star-filled sky and the altruistic spirit of the universe said, "I am here." I felt the snowy ground hold, support and accept me with all my past mistakes and losses. At that moment I heard God say, "Hear me and see me, I have you no matter what." I felt a spiritual awakening enter my heart, mind and soul. My Higher Power had given me hope and love and I finally believed in a power greater than me that could restore me to sanity. And it has—on a daily reprieve.

I now have a great dog walking business. Every day, all day long, I'm with the dogs, nature and my belief that God is leading me in a healthy direction. I remember clearly that night in the snow when I felt entirely safe and held and loved by the spirit of the universe—and that spirit never leaves my side. So to keep the beauty of sobriety, I have a great home group, a gentle sponsor and eager sponsees. But if I go a day without a meeting, or don't work my Steps, the darkness returns quickly. With the help of AA, the Fellowship, and my Higher Power, I have a second chance of a fulfilling life. My heart is mending and becoming more open to love and being loved, to forgiving myself and others...just like Rosco forgave me.

M.N.

Under the Stars
November 2016

When I went camping, I used to take great care in making sure I packed enough alcohol for the trip. Car camping was of course the easiest, as I could bring just about any amount I wanted, and I could drive to get more if I ran low. Backpacking trips took more care, as storage space was at a premium. Several nights out would require substantial amounts of hard liquor, which of course was so difficult to moderate. I would usually bring other drugs to help me get through. I can remember one trip in particular when I didn't bring enough whiskey and ended up arguing with my wife that we had to cut the trip short because my hips hurt, when in fact I was more hurting for liquor.

Today I enjoy camping with my family more than ever. No need to manage liquor. I focus on making sure I have enough food for everyone to be happy and nourished. I pack games that everyone enjoys. I bring my running shoes so that I can get away for a little bit and drain any negative energy that may have accumulated in my system. And I use the quiet moments in between activities to pray and meditate. My Higher Power definitely speaks to me through the nature around me, and I receive some fantastic messages while spending a couple of days in the woods.

Recently, we've even started camping with some friends who also have a family member working to stay sober. I used to rely on booze to calm my nerves and provide entertainment. Now I find the depth of conversations we're able to have over s'mores by the campfire under the stars brings me a serenity and tranquility I never knew. And waking up the next day without a hangover or a fuzzy memory of how I acted a fool the night before is awesome. I'm having more fun than I ever thought possible.

Scott M.
Takoma Park, Md.

Time to Pray
April 2021

I'm a land surveyor by trade. I now enjoy working on the drafting side of the business and rarely make it into the field, but I spent 15 years in the woods taking measurements.

From the extreme wildlife of Louisiana, to the rocky rattlesnake-prone Alabama National Forest lands, to the foothills of the Blue

Mountains in West Virginia, I've been exposed to the wilderness on every level. I've been surrounded by trees my entire life.

Back in 2007, we were painting boundary lines for the Forest Service in Talledega National Forest. Rattlesnakes are very common in steep, rocky terrain and that's exactly where we were. Prior to this experience, I'd had several encounters with snakes, spiders, bees, aggressive bulls, even a rooster pulling some kickboxing maneuver on my leg. Just becomes part of the job.

On this day, we were faced with the presence of rattlesnakes, which are dangerous and potentially deadly. Things can get bad real fast. The guy working with me, Matt, was fairly new and not accustomed to the outdoors. He was very naive to the elements, "green," if you will.

I was walking and paying more attention to the cigarette I was smoking and the equipment I was carrying on my shoulder and to Matt and his inexperience. He was not careful about stepping down from rocks that had a slight overhang that created a "black hole," a perfect spot for a rattlesnake.

Now this particular rock was very typical. Most looked like God threw them into the side of the mountain and they stuck. As we walked, I was taking his Step inventory when I should have been taking my own. From the top of one of these large rocks, I stepped one leg onto the dirt below, right in front of a black hole. I had turned sideways to scale myself down the rock, so at this point I had one leg on top of the rock and one on the ground.

That's when I heard the rattle.

On a steep slope, in an awkward physical twist and with an angry rattlesnake just a few inches from my calf, I suddenly ran out of ideas. Matt, meanwhile, went into panic mode, asking me what to do. I didn't have an answer. I was beyond human aid at that point. So I started praying. The rattle had become so loud and intense it was paralyzing. Keeping the "target" leg still, I slowly shed my backpack. I took the GPS unit off my shoulder and sat down on the rock. I think I even lit another cigarette. After about 10 minutes of not moving, other than an uncontrollable shake, the rattlesnake started to lessen the pace of its frightening rattle. The volume slowly went down as well. Then it just stopped.

I told Matt to walk out in front of the rock to see what she was doing. He told me the snake had backed into the hole, giving me some room, so I picked up my leg and stood up.

Though I didn't know it at the time, this was a powerful First Step-type experience for me. I had a total lack of power in that situation. When I was drinking, my usual reaction to life was (and sometimes still is) based on impulsive emotional reaction. In this case, a sudden panic-laden reaction would've been a fatal mistake. Having had several encounters with snakes, I had obtained just enough wisdom to know better. And I did not suffer a snake bite.

Most decisions I make in emotionally charged situations cause me pain. That tendency to react out of fear or anger was a root cause of my unmanageability. As instinctual as it was for that rattlesnake to rattle when her security was threatened, prayer has become instinctual to me. She rattled by instinct; I prayed by instinct. Prayer seemed natural, even though I was agnostic and had no religious background at the time. I had nowhere to run. I was powerless. Unsure if these prayers would save me, I said them anyway.

And I kept praying when I got sober. Today, the miracles I see happening to me and around me seem natural.

Last week I did my Fifth Step with my sponsor, and he guided me every step of the way. I've never fully understood how he hides his wings in public, but somehow he does. Afterward he walked me out to my car, thanking me for sharing my story with him. When we got to my car, he pointed out the dogwood tree that stood nearby. It was in full flower, which was unusual for Nashville in early spring.

"I've seen thousands of dogwood trees, but I've never seen one that looked like that," he said. Truth be told, between the color of the flowers in the night and the emotional release of having just done the Step, looking at that tree felt comparable to a mushroom trip that nature was putting on for us. I was curious if he, at 27 years sober and having done many Fifth Steps, knew what was going to happen when he pointed out the dogwood tree.

I was amazed by the tree. I thought about how I struggled for a long time with myself and alcohol. I had multiple trips to rehab, multiple stays in sober living homes, multiple early recovery relationships (as my sponsor says, two sick is just too sick), several half-measure attempts at the Steps and numerous geographical changes. The term "fully give myself to the program" was Greek to me when I got sober.

But today I keep my focus on the "right now" and on the gratitude and serenity that come from small miracles in my life like that tree. Some days it's simply showing kindness in every human interaction. Pets too. It seems I have been granted the serenity to do the things I can as a result of this instinct called prayer.

One of my favorite singers is Damien Rice. He has a song named "Cannonball." One of the lyrics, and my personal favorite, says, "It's not hard to grow when you know that you just don't know."

Jonathan H.
Nashville, Tennessee

A Walk in the Park
August 2008

I must confess I'm one of those people who has some trouble with the "God thing." I know many of us do. Sure, the First Step is fairly easy when looking at the powerlessness and damage caused by my alcoholism. But how to get to the Second or Third Steps?

Church just wasn't cutting it. I know some alcoholics have their faith and AA program strengthened by church or temple attendance, but I didn't. I tried for years and nothing really clicked.

What was I going to do? I simply had to do the Second Step to recover from this devastating illness of alcoholism. The God of Nature intervened.

One day I went for a walk in Riding Meadows Park, which was very near one of my favorite meeting places. That's where I came to understand a truly loving, all-powerful God who wants the best for me.

It is so easy to see my Higher Power's handiwork in nature: the quiet creek flowing along, the tadpoles and minnows bubbling along in the shallows, the turtles and frogs. There are the fallen trees that form natural walkways over the creek for many a child to explore. Wildflowers color the path of the park and keep guiding a God-seeker like me further into the natural beauty of my Higher Power's kingdom.

When I go to the park and get out of my own head, the Second Step comes alive. And that is truly the God I've been seeking.

For me, the Second Step wasn't an angst-filled journey; it was a walk in the park.

Rob R.
Oakmont, Pennsylvania

A Fox In the Woods
October 2001

When I tried to apply the Steps of AA to my grief over the death of my 30-year-old daughter, Phyllis, I came to a brick wall. I could admit I was powerless over death. No amount of prayer, bargaining, you-name-it had stopped the inexorable progress of the ovarian cancer that invaded her body, despite surgical intervention and chemotherapy.

Phyllis had attended a spiritual retreat when she was in her early 20s. She told of having something unresolved since the death of her father when she was 16, and she had taken a walk in the woods during the retreat to meditate on this issue. When she had finished her meditation, she asked her Higher Power to give her some sign that her prayer had been heard. As she continued to walk, a fox stepped out of the woods onto the path ahead of her. She stopped walking and watched the fox, who looked at her for a long moment, trotted up the path a few feet, then turned and disappeared into the woods after a backward glance at her.

A few weeks before Phyllis died, her husband was reading to her about the fox from a book on animals and their significance to Native Americans. The book mentioned that the fox is believed by some to be the bearer of messages to and from the spirit world. This was of tremendous significance to Phyllis inasmuch as it confirmed to her that the fox she had seen at the retreat had, indeed, been the sign that her prayer had been heard.

A few months after Phyllis's death, I visited a place near our home where there are rapids along a creek that I frequent when I want to talk to God (I feel less self-conscious talking out loud with the babble of water over the rocks). That day I had something exciting to tell Phyllis. After I had finished, I started to walk away when I added, as an afterthought, "If you heard me, would you please let me see a fox on my way home?" I started up the path toward home, looking left and right to see if there was a fox on one side or the other of the creek, and ahead to see if there was one on the path, but there were no foxes.

Then, just as I was about to turn away from the creek and start up the hill to our house, I glanced to my left one last time and my eyes fell on a sandbar along the creek. There, to my amazement, was a young fox playing with a stick, tossing it up and pouncing on it like a puppy with a toy. He did this several times as I watched, sinking to my knees to thank my Higher Power for this gift.

I go to the rapids often to talk to God and to Phyllis. I don't have to ask for a fox; I know they hear me.

It has been almost five years since Phyllis died. I still miss her and have days when the pain of grief is as fresh as when it was new. These are the days when I am reminded to be grateful that I have a Higher Power to turn to and a program from which to derive the strength to get through another day sober, in spite of my powerlessness over life and death.

Pat S.
Newark, Delaware

Wonderfully Humbling
April 2018

I came into the rooms of AA in 1985 at the age of 52. About four years in, I had a very painful "convincer," which became the foundation for what is now almost 28 years of uninterrupted sobriety. Simply put, I've now been around long enough to know a lifeboat when I'm in one. Obviously, starting to get sober didn't come easy for me. I guess functional alcoholic is the best description of my status as a beginner. I paid our bills, kept food on the table and maintained a roof over our heads.

Looking back, my most obvious mistake was the First Step. I read it as two definitions. Yes, my life had become unmanageable—but powerless over alcohol? No way. Of course, our kids were barely speaking to me. I couldn't negotiate a simple conversation with my wife without raising my voice and bringing her to tears. My business was failing, so I had earned the right to three or five martinis when I got home, to top off my largely liquid lunch. The symptoms of my alcoholism were fairly obvious to anyone who probed a little deeper than my "highly sociable" surface. Things were getting seriously worse for me.

I had a friend who had been in AA for a number of years and his life seemed enviably placid. He was involved in a lot of community activities that seemed to help a broad spectrum of people. He had never broached the subject of alcoholism with me—mine or his—but at some point I asked him how stopping drinking had affected him.

I don't remember all of what got discussed, but I will never forget his appraisal of his experience in AA. It was a mini-qualification followed by a description of how surprised he was that the desire to drink had simply left him. He began to reflect on the self-discovery aspect that comes with time and the added depth to his life. For him, it was a spiritual evolution.

I don't think all of us are bestowed with an instant awareness of a Higher Power in our lives. For many of us, it's AA itself, the kindred fellowship that seems larger than the number of people in any meeting. For me, the awareness came gradually.

I had the immediate task of saving a marriage, a family and a neglected business. I began a steady diet of meetings and got a sponsor with a lot of time in the program. His suggestions (read: mandates) were deliciously simple. The first morsel was: get stupid and reread the Big Book—again. So I did. And I still do.

The ensuing 28 years have not been totally free of speed bumps. There have been emotional potholes, dented egos and several serious prideswipes. Happily, there have been no critical injuries and none of the family appears to be any more— or less—neurotic than the world at large.

Now, long-since retired and enjoying the added geography of 52 years of marriage to the same woman I had brought to tears, I spend part of my mornings out in our backyard, tapping into the incredible serenity that's been there for years and years but which I never noticed. I didn't see it for most of the 50 years I mowed that lawn, but it has become my very own green cathedral.

Our bird feeder seems to be a conduit to my Higher Power. The miraculous activity of our clientele out there produces an instant imponderable: How do they do that? Who designed or engineered all this? The aerodynamics of the bird life is awesome and the magical appearance of a spectacular seasonal change is wonderfully humbling. Obviously, I'm not in charge.

Working in my backyard isn't always an enlightening experience for me, but when the lawn mowers and weedwackers move on and the occasional airliner whispers over the horizon, I get a small window for a one-sided conversation with my Higher Power. He's a good listener. Since I did enough verbal damage in my pre-AA life, I don't feel that requests for absolution are ever in order. I've long since used up all my foxhole prayers.

One day last summer, we heard a knock at our front door. It was a stranger who had been driving by and had to stop for two bear cubs crossing the road. We each had the same question: Could mama bear be far away?

We thanked him for the alert and promptly called our neighbors down the hill who have small children who often play outside. They were called inside and a vigil began. Past dusk, we heard nothing and had no sightings of any wildlife except the chipmunks and squirrels policing the area under the bird feeder. Things remained quiet until well after dark.

We are apparently pretty sound sleepers, because the following morning we discovered the bird feeder, flattened on the ground. A second, satellite feeder had suffered the same fate. The metal pole from which they'd hung was bent to a 90-degree angle where it stood. Mama bear could be an NFL draft pick. I took my usual meditation chair on the patio and began to swear. I think I may have set a record for unrepeatable profanity.

Finally, I ran out of four-letter words and it got quiet. I sat there. I couldn't hear mowers or air traffic. The most profound serenity I've ever felt enveloped me.

I'm not sure how long I sat there and I don't know if I heard a "voice" or words flowed across the empty page my mind had become, but somehow, some way, I got a message. It was this: "That bear is one of my creatures too, pal."

Sometimes quickly, sometimes slowly...

Dick C.
New City, New York

Perfect Timing
May 2015

I got sober in 1964, when I was 29 years old, and have remained sober since that time. When I was new in sobriety, in addition to attending many meetings, one of the first things I got involved in was gardening. I don't recall anyone saying I had a "green thumb," but I spent a lot of time moving dirt and seeds around. One time, in my wisdom, I decided to leave the green beans one more day before harvesting them. When I returned to the garden, I had—as AA members would say—a learning experience: rabbits, woodchucks, you name it, had chosen to not wait for the next day and did the harvesting on their own. So no green beans for me. I learned that timing is invaluable, and that I must take each day as it comes.

There is a time to plant, and a time to harvest. Gardening is controlled by water and sunshine. Cloudy days are opportunities to transplant because the roots are safe from the sun's rays. Once again, timing is everything. Every serious gardener has their own rules and ways of doing things, but all involve applying water and sun—and lots of love. That's how we get to know everything about our gardens.

I started to notice that one bird spent a lot of time on a side hill, maybe 15 to 20 yards from my garden. There were a lot of cats, rabbits, dogs and squirrels moving around, in addition to the nocturnal raccoons, skunks, possums and other creatures of the night. As I watched the bird, I came to the conclusion that it was not injured. So I knew enough to keep a distance from whatever the bird was doing. In time, I learned the bird had built a nest on the ground. I had read in one of my bird books that this was not uncommon: it meant the bird and chicks had immunity from giving off a scent for a certain length of time.

Up to that point, it had been impossible for me to grasp how God takes care of his creations in many different ways. Well, all I needed to do was to accept. I couldn't doubt anymore because I was seeing it with my own eyes.

Eventually the chicks grew and flew away, as did the mother bird. A couple of days later, the cats discovered the nest and destroyed it. So there had been a time to hatch and then a time to leave. I was fascinated. This to me was another example of God's love.

Obviously, the birds became a bigger show for me than the garden had been. It's only for a short time that flowers bloom, vegetables grow and ripen. Gardens bring great joy: as we get in touch with Mother Earth, it brings us closer to ourselves.

I often wonder if I would have become as attentive to the rhythms of nature had the green beans not been eaten by the animals. The bird with her inner wisdom and perfect timing showed me a wink from God. I could sense the trust of the chicks in their mom without hesitation. The wisdom of the mother bird had taught me to believe in a power greater than myself. In that moment, doubt had no place in me. I witnessed nature's perfect balance that told the little birds precisely when it was time to leave the nest.

Alcoholics Anonymous carries me daily with patient love. It teaches me that one day at a time is where it's at.

Bob D.
Haverhill, Massachusetts

PART II

Techniques & Practices

There are many ways to pray and meditate

As recounted by AA's cofounder Bill W. in the Step Eleven chapter of the book *Twelve Steps and Twelve Traditions*, "In AA we have found that the actual good results of prayer are beyond question. They are matters of knowledge and experience." And, of meditation he added, "It is essentially an individual adventure, something which each one of us works out in his own way."

The AA members in this chapter each have their own perspective on prayer and meditation—how they do it and what it means to them on a daily basis. For Rick P., in the story "A Sacred Safari," meditation has been like "a sacred safari into myself, where I was never quite sure what to expect once I dared to venture into my inner, deeper spiritual jungle." Ken T. in his article "Binge Thinker," writes, "Once I learned to meditate...I was able to find the 'off' switch to my thinking."

For E.P., in the story "Divine Hot Line," turning from formal prayer to conversational prayer was freeing. "I could talk to God in simple, direct, and truthful terms, in everyday language, and the more I practiced this, the more I began to understand the admonition to 'practice the presence of God.'"

In her story "Spending Time with God," Emily G. brings the book to a close, writing, "The best part about Step Eleven is that there is no wrong way to do it.... There is no magical formula, book or equation on how to achieve this. I've found a way that works for me, and in return I'm able to find God no matter where I am in my day."

Highest Form of Prayer
January 1987

I spent 47 years talking to myself, trusting myself, relying on my own best judgment. My best judgment finally brought me to my knees. I was defeated, miserable and hopelessly addicted. For me, there were three painkillers in life—alcohol, drugs and sex. I liked all three, I'd take two, but I had to have one! My daily fix.

God has done for me what I could not do for myself. He has taken this defect of character and changed it for me. He took my weakness and turned it into the most powerful asset I have today. God has given me the ability to talk to him, to listen to him for guidance in my daily life, and the willingness to follow his directions.

Meditation is my new daily "fix." When I meditate, I ask God questions. I keep it simple, and I listen for his answer. What usually happens is that I realize I am in a thought process, and this process is God's way of telling me what he wants me to do. It blows my mind!

For me, meditation is the highest form of prayer. I turn my will and my life over to God every time I ask him a question, listen for the answer, and become willing to set aside my fears and act on that "gut feeling" I get.

There are other forms of prayer that I use daily. I pray for others, especially when I become resentful toward them. I pray in gratitude, for I now realize that everything I have today is a gift from God. I do not pray selfishly for anything for myself, because I have come to believe that the Big Book is right—it doesn't work.

There was a time when I couldn't meditate. I now realize it was my own fear of what the answers might be that prevented me from conscious contact with my Higher Power. I have learned to walk through these fears, from the bridge of reason to the desired shore of faith.

I prefer talking to God for guidance these days, instead of talking to myself. My life is still a soap opera, and I'm still the star. The exciting difference is that I now have a new director. Meditation is still the best "medication" I've ever had—for everything that ails me!

J. V.
Aspen, Colorado

Lost—and Found—at Sea
December 1987

T he entire trip was turning into a disaster. Not only had the atmosphere between my husband and me been tense in the hotel room, but now we were arguing in public and in front of the children. I saw the fear in their eyes.

Swallowing the despair in my throat, I scooted for the stairway to the deck of the ferryboat we were on, trying to get away from the looks people were giving me—and from him. Once up top, the crisp wind dried those tears and I took a deep breath and began trying to ignore the situation.

"Look, kids," I said briskly, "look at the gulls following the boat. Did you bring the bread we saved?"

Just then I felt my husband's hand on my elbow. "Let's talk," he said. A rush of hatred poured through me. I jerked my arm away angrily and began to stride down the deck.

"No," I spat back at him. "I'm going to meditate."

I went to the rear of the boat and sat on a bench where not too many people were passing by. I knew I had to shut off the clamor of voices in my head. Every voice had something bitter to say, and most of them were telling me what I should have said back to him.

I began the two-part process I had come to understand as meditation: first, shutting off my own mind, then relaxing to allow the message in—intuitions or healing which I had been told would come.

Half an hour later, I found myself coming out of the meditation burbling with laughter. None of that is important, was the thought in my mind, none of that is important at all. I chuckled to myself and shook my head with amusement at how caught up in it I had been. But none of that is important, I repeated once again.

When I rejoined my family, I was full of good humor. As the weekend wore on, the mood lasted. As we drove back across two states to our home, I glanced at my husband, amused.

"I'll bet you're wondering what's going on," I queried, patting his knee affectionately. He admitted that he hadn't wanted to disturb the calm by questioning me.

"I don't know what happened during that meditation," I said, "because I can't remember most of the 20 minutes. All I know is that something must have healed inside me." My husband just shook his head in grateful amazement.

At the time this occurred, despite quite a few years of recovery in the Fellowship, I was still a miserable person, driven by unhappiness and an unsatisfactory relationship. I felt I had worked the program tirelessly, but depression was eroding my hard-won sense of well-being. A sponsor's question prompted me to realize that I had never consistently done the Eleventh Step. I was awkward about using these spiritual tools, but a willingness to change must have made up for my inexperience.

The event was surely a tiny miracle and once demonstrated, I could never forget the possibility of such healing. In these past years, I have grown slowly into the belief that life is good, and so are all the things that happen in it.

The relationship did finally resolve itself, but more important was my newly learned ability to live contented and free from my own negative feelings during the time of working it through.

I thought it was the marriage that needed to be fixed in order to make me happy; I learned instead to be happy regardless of the situations around me. The primary tool which made that freedom possible was meditation.

I have learned that meditation is not praying or reading, and that it is more than just listening—it's receiving. It was hard to learn because my mind wanted to be in charge, but I trained it to turn off and the effort has been well worth it. Meditation has become a reprieve from all the necessary mental activity which keeps out the quieter source with which I need to keep in touch. My life contains so many little joys these days. Meditating has become one of them, and its regular practice helps keep me present with all the others.

D. T.
Billings, Montana

A Sacred Safari
April 2004

T he stress of learning to meditate really shocked me. Maybe it was a control issue. Prayer seemed easier, probably because I felt in control over how I prayed or what I prayed for. Meditation, however, was like a sacred safari into myself, where I was never quite sure what to expect once I dared to venture into my inner, deeper spiritual jungle. That may be too melodramatic, but the discouraging reality was that for many years the meditation suggested in the Eleventh Step was a divine mind-maze to me.

My quest began with my sponsor's suggestion that meditation might help a newcomer like me to manage my unmanageable mind. He kept it simple, explaining, "Prayer is talking to God, and meditation is listening to God." Easiest thing in the world, I thought. So after a quick self-centered prayer, I began listening for God's voice. Unfortunately, years of drinking had drowned it out and replaced it with my own wild imagination. Thoughts of justifiable vengeance, grandiose accomplishments, and delusions of universal adoration flooded my ego-driven meditations in those first few years. Eventually, to avoid temptations born of frustration, I gave up. But I didn't drink, so I was free to try again a few years later.

By the time I'd been sober a decade, my conscious contact had slipped into a coma, so I decided to give this "meditation thing" another shot. This time, I tried "T.M.," transcendental meditation, a technique I recalled from the blurred memories of my hippie period, when I was drinking and knew everything. I innocently envisioned the joy of having T.M. clear my mind of all thoughts and taking me to a higher spiritual plane on the way to cosmic serenity. Unfortunately, while my spirit was meditating, my brain was hesitating. The bees were a constant distraction: the ought-to-bees, could-bees, should-bees and wannabees were merciless. Another problem with T.M. was my search for a mantra, a one-syllable word that helps the mind to focus on nothing. I realized I was having a mantra meltdown when the only word that echoed in my consciousness was "beer." Shortly thereafter, I gave up again.

A few years later, still sober but shaken by life on life's terms, I reached back to my religious heritage and pulled out my beads. With a few AA adjustments, I found them quite comforting. The repetition and structure of the prayers helped me stay focused until my archenemy, boredom, led me astray into the hunt for the perfect way. One particularly frenzied day, while I was praying desperately in the shower, the beads broke and I watched them and my efforts slide right down the drain. It was then that I realized I might want to reread Step Eleven in the "Twelve and Twelve" to see what I'd missed.

A decade later, I finally hit upon a system that comfortably blended the simplicity of the program with the complexity of my personality to create a manageable mode of meditation. It's called RAP. RAP may sound incongruous for a middle-aged, white suburbanite until you know that for me RAP stands for "reflect and ponder." Each day after I pray, with God as my guide, I gently allow myself to reflect on any experience that floats into my mind. No longer weighed down with guilt, I can allow a feeling of guilt to float in and float out and feel blessed by its visit. When I'm not reflecting, I ponder the good "yets" that could happen if I don't get drunk today. The awareness that they are possibilities and not guarantees keep my meditations honest, hopeful, sober and sane.

One reflection revealed how often I had craved spiritual complexity over the years, a kind of spiritual self-importance born of alcoholic insecurity. I'm grateful that the program, the love of the people in the meetings, and the grace of God have taught me that most complicated ideas are authored by us humans. God may share profound revelations, but he usually uses little words. Simplicity is harder for some than for others. I think meditation is that way, too. But for those willing to persevere, I believe God is willing to wait till we embrace him within the silence.

Rick P.
Vernon, Connecticut

Conscious Contact
November 1991

When I first joined AA I was an atheist and unable to pray. After attending 90 meetings in 90 days, I knelt by my bed one morning and in tearful frustration pounded with my fists and cried, "If you are up there, if there is a God, help me!" In the days to follow I tried to meditate and pray, but I really didn't know how. Like many newcomers, the idea of meditation or prayer seemed too esoteric for me, something only priests or pastors could do. Gradually I was able to learn, through reading, and through much practice, to "let go and let God." But it took some doing!

There are many techniques and methods of meditation, from saying the rosary to doing yoga asanas. Inward repetition of a prayer or a mantra is one way. There is always some self-discipline involved, but it does work. One way or another, one's emotional balance and stimulated intuition begin to stir.

My way is consciously to relax each muscle in my body, one by one, sitting in a straight chair, breathing deeply while rolling my eyes back under closed lids and feeling my body heavy against the chair, my

hands loose in my lap. I control my desire to look at the clock and I ignore "drunken monkey thoughts." I pay attention to how I am feeling.
If I am angry or resentful, I pay attention to that. If I don't know "what
to do today," I look at that and I ask God to send me answers. Perhaps
today I should do nothing but go to a meeting. If I empty myself and
let God in it is working.

Gradually a sense of freedom and light permeates my being. Clarity
and love of God are there and fear departs. The process does not need
to be understood to allow it to happen.

Later, when I open my eyes, what a sensation it is to look around
me and see that nothing has changed. I am still in the same body, the
same room, the same house, the same world. But I have acquired conscious contact with God as I understand him. I can pause during the
day for only a second, ask for help, or say "Thank you!" God goes with
me all day. Now I turn my life and will over to him every morning. (I
have been sober 13 years.) Step Eleven is the maintenance I need to
expand my awareness of the world of God's good.

Jeanie N.
Napa, California

Binge Thinker
July 2010

Before I was powerless over alcohol and my life had become
unmanageable, I was powerless over unhappiness and my
life had become unmanageable. I turned to alcohol in my
late 40s as the best self-help option I thought I could find. Often,
my unhappiness seemed to melt as I drank. But drinking became an
ever more elusive and flawed solution to my unhappiness. It began to
create unhappiness of its own. My overall unhappiness was eventually much greater than what I had evaded and yet not solved at the
beginning of my alcoholism. Now what?

Maybe the best way to feel was to be happy. How was that possible?

Long before I was a binge drinker, I was a binge thinker. I tended to think incessantly, as if this were an essential part of staying alive. My mind either had no "off" switch, or if it did, I had no idea where it was. In this constant banter, I could find all sorts of resentments to chew on, grudges to hold, victimizations to ponder and catastrophes to protest. Life was unfair, people were the harbingers of much injustice and unkindness, and I was justifiably withholding my seal of approval by not accepting what already was.

I create thoughts. I can do so from default behaviors (what I have come to otherwise recognize as "character defects"), or I can create thoughts within the awareness of having choices. Awareness for me is realizing that I am not my thoughts. Rather, I observe my thoughts and their creation and content. If I need not be run by my conditioned default thinking, then have I discovered the choice of observing and creating constructive thinking?

Once I learned to meditate, as encouraged in Step Eleven, I was able to find the "off" switch to my thinking when that thinking is neither needed nor useful to me. I can use thought, rather than have my thinking use me. "Awareness," I believe, is the most accessible doorway to what has been referred to as "spirituality" throughout my life and in AA.

Ken T.
Ames, Iowa

Staying in the Day
April 2021

The Eleventh Step is my favorite. That's because my connection with my Higher Power has been an ongoing unfoldment throughout my sobriety.

When I first got to AA 21 years ago, all I could see was destruction around me, as I had lost everything. Looking back, I know now that God was doing for me what I could not do for myself.

Before AA, when my focus was on everything except my Higher Power, I couldn't see how I was destroying my life. It came with a heavy price. I lost my home and my family. I found myself in the back of an empty church in the dark, crying out to God for help. I looked around and saw all the candles and I recalled how, when I was little, I used to light the candles and pray for loved ones. Would that work for me now? I saw that I needed help and comfort. Luckily, I found my way to AA.

Today, my meditation practice includes writing. I'll take a page and write "It's a brand new, never before lived, baby day! This is the most authentic and loving year of my life, so far."

Writing this out gives me a feeling that I am fully in the day and full of gratitude. I have stacks and stacks of these pages, all starting with the same message, but different days, all written out.

I can look back on these days with love because I not only thought in gratitude, but also wrote it down.

Then at night I reflect on my day and do an inventory of my "wins." I focus on instances when I was kind, generous or gave someone a hand. By focusing on my wins, I then consciously create more wins for the next day. If I mess up, I go back and correct my wrongs and count that as a win.

Conscious contact throughout the day is also important for me. I keep meditation music on in the background, which calms me down as I drive to my AA meetings.

This is my daily process. It's not perfect, but it does offer a method to stay focused on the Steps all through the day—a segue into Step Twelve, one meditation at a time.

Judy M.
Leander, Texas

Believing
January 1980

U nderstanding something about God and accepting him have been, and still are, experiences of considerable magnitude in my life. Even now, I'm not sure how much I understand, but acceptance is no longer a problem. Whatever degree of understanding I have has come slowly and gradually, over an extended period of time. Thanks to the AA program, I'm not impatient nor am I discouraged.

As a young person, I was taught right from wrong, and I was taught there was a God. I never rebelled and said there wasn't a God, nor did I turn against him. To me, it just didn't seem to make any difference, one way or the other. Even during my worst drinking days, I felt there was a God, but I didn't have time for that. I tied God in with religion, and I was less than enthusiastic about religion. I felt that it was my responsibility to work out my own living problems, and I couldn't see any reason why I should ask God for help.

Before coming to AA, I didn't know how to live and work with the idea of a Higher Power. I didn't know about the help and guidance that God could give me in my daily life. I didn't know it was through prayer that I could receive his help. I didn't even know how to pray; I always felt inadequate, because the prayers that I had heard were rather formally and eloquently offered by men of the cloth. I have no complaint against formal and eloquent prayers, but they aren't nearly as meaningful to me as the prayers that I say today, in the plain and simple words that I use in my everyday life, the same words that I use in sharing with my fellow man.

Every day, and at any time of the day, I can now share with God. If I'm happy, disturbed or uncertain which way to turn, I can share it with my Higher Power. I know there is a must: I must be honest in my sharing. If I'm sincere in asking for guidance, it will be given to me, if I keep it simple and on a level that I understand.

How did this acceptance of God come about? It came about through the willingness to listen, to share, and to read. The result of these has been that I came to believe—believe in prayer and believe in God.

C. B.
Santa Maria, California

Alcoholic's Meditation
November 2010

After several years of regular attendance at an Eleventh Step study, a simple meditation came to me that I think of as the "alcoholic's meditation." With each in-breath, I think, Welcome. With each out-breath, I think, Thank you. That leaves me fluctuating between acceptance and gratitude, which I recognize as two of the integral principles of Alcoholics Anonymous. Although my sobriety is based on faith in God, this simple meditation can work for agnostics and atheists as well, who can readily practice acceptance and gratitude without necessarily believing in God. Like so many things in AA, this meditation works when I work it. By welcoming God into my day and then thanking him for being in it, this meditation continually blesses me.

Ed L.
Wrightwood, California

Many Powers Greater Than Me
February 2019

When I came into AA, I was a nonbeliever, or so I thought. I struggled all my life with the concept of God. I believe in the existence of God so I know I'm not an atheist. I know from my own experiences that the existence of God is knowable so I'm not agnostic either. I'm not sure what I am…and I'm not sure it really matters. But I knew I needed a Higher Power to work the Steps and stay sober.

I tried using the group as my Higher Power, but I found that I couldn't pray to my group. My sponsor wanted me to take certain actions, whether I believed in them or not, and one of those actions was praying. So I got on my knees every morning and asked something to help me stay sober and I thanked that something every night.

I learned over time, with the help of my sponsor, that I wasn't really a nonbeliever. I was just very angry with God because my daddy died when I was a little girl. I chose to stop believing in God because things just happened, there was no one to blame and no reasons to search for. It was easier not to believe.

My sponsor pointed out that I couldn't be angry at something that didn't exist. That was a light bulb moment and it opened my eyes and my mind to be willing to believe.

With some time and personal experience, that anger began to fade. As I stayed sober and life got better, I began to believe that that "something" I prayed to was God. I felt God much more in my head than in my heart.

It was suggested that I try to seek God in order to develop the sort of personal relationship I wanted with God and had heard other AA members talking about. I worked hard trying to do that. I looked for him in nature. I looked for him in those small coincidences, and I went to church for the first three years of my sobriety.

The God they talked about in church was different from the God I heard about in meetings. Church ended up provoking more questions than it provided answers. I had the belief, but very little, or no, faith. I still didn't know if God heard or answered my prayers. I didn't know what God did or didn't do. I didn't know what his part was and what part was mine. But I did know that God brought me to AA. I knew he wanted me to stay here and that he gave me the strength I needed to stay.

Even though I'm not sure he hears or answers my prayers, I keep praying. I keep taking the actions. I talk to him all day. I ask him for help. I bring him my fears and concerns and I ask him to give me strength. I even share my doubts with him. Just taking the actions without faith calms my fears, provides relief and brings some peace.

I know God loves me even though I may never be able to feel that in my heart. My lack of faith has kept me up at night wondering if what I do have is good enough to keep me sober. I learned I don't have to have all the answers, but I have found a way that works for me.

To me, depending on a Higher Power just means I have a source outside of myself that I can go to, depend on and trust more than I trust myself. I need to acknowledge that I can't do this alone, that I need help to stay sober and to make my life manageable. So, I pray to God.

I have a sponsor who I can see, hear and trust. I have friends to help me through the rough times and to share the good times. I need all of them to stay sober and they are all powers greater than me. I have five years of sobriety now so I know it works. And I believe it will continue to work one day at a time, as long as I know that I am not God and that I can't do this deal alone.

Judy E.
Orland Park, Illinois

Sitting in Silence, Listening
November 2009

In early sobriety it was suggested to me that I think of prayer as talking to God and meditation as listening. That idea took hold. I sobered up in 1972; in 1984 I learned how to meditate at a Catholic retreat center, under a priest who had spent 25 years in Japan studying Zen Buddhism. That was my introduction to the practice of meditation, and it took.

In 1985 I was down and out with chronic fatigue, so I began a meditation meeting in my home, mostly to get myself up and out of bed. My group, mostly local women alcoholics, met from 7 to 7:30 A.M., Monday through Friday. There was no talking. It was just sitting in silence, listening, for 30 minutes. At 7:30 I'd gong a gong and we'd all stand in a circle and bow, using the word "namaste", which means "I honor the divine in you." They'd leave and I'd go back to bed.

It's now years later and I'm into my sixth year of healing from chronic fatigue. I believe that there's a touch of good in every single thing. The biggest gift of living with chronic fatigue for 19 years is that I became dedicated to meditation—to listening to God—and I learned how to quiet my mind. The morning meditation ended a few years ago, but a Wednesday night meditation group continues. The best gift of meditation, from my perspective, is that I've been introduced to the Spirit of the Universe by experiencing it in the very breath that I breathe. I love that God is available to all equally, that he's all about love, and that some of us experience that source of love by simply practicing the AA principles in all our affairs.

Linda I.
El Granada, California

First Things First
November 1991

A   t 7:00 A.M. five days a week you can find a small group of
       AAs meeting at a club on the north side of Tallahassee,
       Florida. The group is called Conscious Contact. Its purpose
is the daily practice of the Eleventh Step.

The meeting usually starts with a reading from the Eleventh Step discussion in the Big Book that begins "On awakening let us think about the twenty-four hours ahead." Then the Serenity Prayer begins a 25 minute period of silent meditation. Meditation ends with the prayer of St. Francis from the Eleventh Step in the "Twelve and Twelve." A brief discussion follows. After the Lord's Prayer we're off to work at 7:45.

The meeting has been going for about a year now. For those of us who attend, it has become an essential part of our lives. In the "Twelve and Twelve" Bill W. compares meditation to food and water. In our experience the comparison is appropriate.

Out of this meeting has developed a method for directly dealing with resentment, frustration and fear. The meditation-based approach is a powerful addition to the technique suggested in the story "Freedom from Bondage" in the Big Book. It is an alternative for people who never learned to pray or don't like prayer.

Meditation is a little like playing a musical instrument. Anyone can make a sound with a violin but it takes practice to make music with one. Just a few days of regular practice will provide benefits. Two weeks of daily meditation, at the same time each day, should show tangible changes in the quality of your life.

There are a number of introductory books on meditation at most bookstores and libraries. For the first year of my meditation practice all I did was count my breaths—one to 10 and then back to one. This is a good way to quiet the committee meeting going on in your head.

The book *Zen Training* by K. Sekida has some very good instruction on meditation and breathing. His basic breathing exercise is "bamboo" breathing, or breathing in segments: Breathe in in three stages—breathe, pause, breathe, pause, breathe, pause. Breathe out in one stage against slight pressure. It will take a little practice to get the pressure right. If you're gasping for breath the exhalation pressure is too high. If the pressure is too low there will be little tension in your abdomen and your mind will tend to wander.

The idea is to keep tension in your lower abdomen while you are breathing. If you do this, you can keep your mind tightly focused. Sekida also suggests focusing on an object and holding your breath for a minute while maintaining the focus. You will find that it is much easier to hold your mind focused if you also hold your breath. You may want to start with 15 or 20 seconds and work up to a full minute. This technique has added to the quality of my meditation in terms of clarity of mind.

The procedure for eliminating resentment, frustration and fear uses the segmented breathing technique. First, you bring the cause of your resentment or frustration, or the object of your fear, clearly into mind. You attempt to experience it in detail. Then you abruptly return to your inmost self by closing your eyes and focusing your eyes and mind on an infinite wall while practicing deep abdominal breathing using the segmented technique. Ten minutes of this practice can blow away small resentments.

An example of the power of mindfulness came to me last year. One day my secretary told me in an excited way that there would be a meeting the next day during which the transfer of some of my space to other people would be discussed. This came in the midst of trying to rebuild an alcohol devastated life. After assuring her that there would be no conflict, I went on with my work. But by the time I got home at 5:15 I felt attacked, and feelings I have learned to recognize as depression were very strong. It got worse. At 5:30 I used the bamboo breathing exercises to return to my inmost self. By 5:40 I was back to normal, not to be bothered again. Four years ago this event could have lasted for a month and I would have been physically ill for the entire time. (As it turned out, the meeting didn't even get to a discussion of my space.)

Seven o'clock in the morning is a tough time for most alcoholics, active or recovering. It took me three months to get to the point where I could look forward to getting to a 7:00 A.M. meeting five days a week. The benefits have been considerable. The use of segmented breathing and mindfulness to deal with fear and resentment is just one benefit. The practice has brought serenity into my life that was previously unimagined.

Solitary meditation is excellent, but meditation in a group is even better. There is something about the power of the group that helps keep my mind from wandering and makes me more open to my Higher Power.

If you get to Tallahassee, come to see us for the early-morning meeting. For those who come, it is a solid experience on which to start the day. People who come daily for two weeks tend to come back for a long time.

Ralph D.
Tallahassee, Florida

Divine Hot Line
December 1977

From time to time at closed AA meetings, when someone shares his closeness and contact with the God of his understanding, a person sitting next to me has whispered, "He sounds as if he has a hotline to God!" This remark is usually tinged with sarcasm and disbelief.

Recently, when someone said this to me, I kept thinking about it as I drove home and found myself saying, "I do, indeed, have a hotline to my God, and I would not survive without it."

I came to AA bringing a mixture of philosophy, psychology, logic, science and theology so confusing as to put me into the category of an agnostic with mental and spiritual indigestion. The God I understood then was a frightening entity, separate and apart from me. I had no regular communication with that entity, nor did I give it much thought or feel any need to make its acquaintance. I was "doing my own thing" long before it became popular to say or do so, and this willfulness was leading me into all kinds of trouble and into alcoholism, with its ultimate consequences of destruction—death or insanity.

In my family, there were a number of ministers of two denominations, but I had failed dogma, orthodoxy and creed. Religions had not failed me; it was I who could not conform to them. Yet all along I had been studying, reading and talking with others, searching for the meaning of life. The eternal mysteries of birth, life and death persistently plagued me when I was faced with problems. I longed for answers and some meaning to my life.

Not until my disease of alcoholism was full-blown and the crash landing came did I realize for the first time that I was powerless and that those who loved me were powerless to help me. Admitting and accepting this fact, I turned myself over to AA and soon was praying lamely, "Whatever God is helping these people, please help me." With this simple prayer, uttered time and again, and an almost monotonous repetition of the Serenity Prayer, there entered into my life a presence that had not been there before. This presence came during one of my quiet times, which I disciplined myself to have early each morning before dressing for work. Something loving, gentle, tender and beautiful came to abide with me. I felt this powerful presence to be God.

I had brought a lot of troubles to AA with me—broken relationships, a lost business, financial problems, a job that was in danger of being lost, no close friends and no family nearby. Alone in an efficiency apartment, I found myself talking to this God in the same language I am using now. At first, it seemed a little crazy to be talking out loud to this unseen friend. But since I lived alone, there was no one to question my sanity. I poured out my feelings, my fears, my despair and my disappointment in myself and others. This was an ordinary conversation, not conventional prayer. I was talking to a loving, caring, all-powerful friend, and I was reassured and comforted.

For almost five years, I prayed for specifics. All of these prayers were answered in the right way—yes, no, maybe, wait—but I could not see the rightness of some answers, especially the "no" answers, until I looked at them in retrospect. In time, I understood that if I turned my will and my life over to the God I was making my companion, some of my answers would have to be no for my highest good, and for the highest good of others.

Turning from formal prayer—the "thee and thou" traditional way of praying in my childhood—to conversational prayer was a great freedom for me. I could talk to God in simple, direct and truthful terms, in everyday language, and the more I practiced this, the more I began to understand the admonition to "practice the presence of God." The thank-yous were audibly or silently expressed many times a day, in gratitude for the unexpected answers, the blessings, and yes, even the trials that allowed for my growth. There were small prayers for others I might see as I walked or drove along—for people who seemed troubled or ill or handicapped or just plainly joyful.

I stopped giving a list to God when I fully understood Step Eleven's "praying only for knowledge of His will for us and the power to carry that out." I could still give thanks for God's love, and pray for sobriety, guidance, protection, healing and enlightenment; but no longer did I draw a description of what I thought I wanted. My faith in my Higher Power grew so that I trusted God to manage my affairs and became willing to accept his will for me.

As time went on, I felt the need for more. Meditation replaced contemplation in the quiet times I set aside each day. Friends more advanced in this practice taught me how to enter into this, one of man's oldest methods of worship, for a time of quieting the body and the mind and putting myself in a mood receptive to inspiration, and for a time, at the end of the meditation periods, for offering up prayers for others who were sick or suffering or having trouble getting sober. I prayed for their highest good, not asking for specific results. And I always remembered Bill W.'s suggestion that when guidance seemed to be strong, we check it out with another trusted AA friend. This safeguard is a necessary one to prevent my ego from stepping in and rationalizing something I might want.

A hotline, as I understand it, is an immediate connection for communication. I can use mine anywhere, any time. I do not hear a thunderous voice in response, but if I wait and listen and observe, replies will come, often in many unexpected and surprising ways. Inspiration or answers may come through the words of a friend or a stranger; a sudden insight may come without effort on my part—in something I am reading, in something someone says at a meeting, or in my dream sleep.

In my hotline conversation, one-sided as it seems, I present my problems or concerns, cite my options as I can see them, and then turn them over to God. When I have done this, I try to let the problems go mentally.

There are times when I find conditions and situations so disturbing that I cannot pray about them. All I can say on my hotline is "God help me"; but this is a powerful prayer. That prayer and the prayers of others have brought me through the pain of death of loved ones, the trauma of early retirement on disability, operations, illness in the deep of night when all the world seems to be asleep and far away. But the hotline is always open, always there. It is the greatest source of comfort and security I have—the feeling that my loving Higher Power is always there, ready to comfort, to show the way, to love me without demand.

E.P.
Alexandria, Virginia

Spending Time With God
November 2016

For the first year of my sobriety, I could only whisper a short "Please help me stay sober today" and finish my day with a simple "Thank you." On days when I was feeling especially powerless over my alcoholism, I resorted to begging God to help me not drink for the next five minutes, hour or afternoon. I often said emergency prayers and tried using God to save the day. I said a lot of prayers that really were orders in disguise for God to give me what I wanted or thought I needed and deserved.

While some oldtimers said I needed to "try harder to talk to God," this was all I could muster at the time. I lived in fear and rolled my eyes at the members who spoke of their "deep conversations with God." What a joke, I thought. All the while, a pit in my stomach longed for a more direct linkage and connection to something greater.

I'm grateful it was suggested that I take the Steps in order. This allowed me to begin to understand what I needed in a Higher Power and what that could look like. Initially, God was very limited in my finite mind to a spirit that could simply love me unconditionally and keep me safe. As I progressed through the Steps, I began to trust in something outside of myself. I began to have a book of God moments and God signs that made it harder to doubt that there was something else out there.

One of my biggest dilemmas the first time through the Steps was how afraid I was of prayer and meditation. I had long been a perfectionist, which worked quite well when I was in the world of academia. But this long-standing personality trait (or defect) was keeping up a high wall between the God of my understanding and me. I had immense fear that I would pray "incorrectly" and God would not be able to hear me. I truly believed that other AA members had access to some sort of secret prayer and meditation manual that instructed them how to properly pray, meditate, talk to and hear direction straight from God. My ego interfered with my ability to ask questions of how other members performed Step Eleven in their daily lives. And I was afraid to share with my friends what prayer and meditation looked like for me—in case I was doing it "wrong."

The best part about Step Eleven is that there is no wrong way to do it. Step Eleven encourages me to speak to God through prayer and listen to God via meditation. There is no magical formula, book or equation on how to achieve this. I've found a way that works for me, and in return I'm able to find God no matter where I am in my day. God and I have frequent chats, apart from a formal recitation of prayers or elaborate readings from my meditation books. Instead, it's just a conversation about my fears, my excitement, my concerns and my stories that take place while walking into coffee shops, driving my car, sitting on my bed, or swimming laps. I've had to make God bigger over the years, so that he could be more involved and enter into all areas of my life.

I've learned that I cannot just ask God to reveal his will to me, but I also have to listen closely to hear the answer. Today, I'm able to ask God to use me how he wants. Prayer is no longer about trying to get God to change his will to make me happy. Rather, it's about finding out what his will is so that I can align myself with his purpose for me in the world. I now have a deep trust and faith in my Higher Power. It gives me great comfort in knowing that for today, I'll be provided with everything I need.

Emily G.
Paradise Valley, Arizona

The Twelve Steps

1. We admitted we were powerless over alcohol—that our lives had become unmanageable.
2. Came to believe that a Power greater than ourselves could restore us to sanity.
3. Made a decision to turn our will and our lives over to the care of God *as we understood Him.*
4. Made a searching and fearless moral inventory of ourselves.
5. Admitted to God, to ourselves, and to another human being the exact nature of our wrongs.
6. Were entirely ready to have God remove all these defects of character.
7. Humbly asked Him to remove our shortcomings.
8. Made a list of all persons we had harmed, and became willing to make amends to them all.
9. Made direct amends to such people wherever possible, except when to do so would injure them or others.
10. Continued to take personal inventory and when we were wrong promptly admitted it.
11. Sought through prayer and meditation to improve our conscious contact with God *as we understood Him,* praying only for knowledge of His will for us and the power to carry that out.
12. Having had a spiritual awakening as the result of these steps, we tried to carry this message to alcoholics, and to practice these principles in all our affairs.

The Twelve Traditions

1. Our common welfare should come first; personal recovery depends upon A.A. unity.
2. For our group purpose there is but one ultimate authority—a loving God as He may express Himself in our group conscience. Our leaders are but trusted servants; they do not govern.
3. The only requirement for A.A. membership is a desire to stop drinking.
4. Each group should be autonomous except in matters affecting other groups or A.A. as a whole.
5. Each group has but one primary purpose—to carry its message to the alcoholic who still suffers.
6. An A.A. group ought never endorse, finance or lend the A.A. name to any related facility or outside enterprise, lest problems of money, property and prestige divert us from our primary purpose.
7. Every A.A. group ought to be fully self-supporting, declining outside contributions.
8. Alcoholics Anonymous should remain forever nonprofessional, but our service centers may employ special workers.
9. A.A., as such, ought never be organized; but we may create service boards or committees directly responsible to those they serve.
10. Alcoholics Anonymous has no opinion on outside issues; hence the A.A. name ought never be drawn into public controversy.
11. Our public relations policy is based on attraction rather than promotion; we need always maintain personal anonymity at the level of press, radio and films.
12. Anonymity is the spiritual foundation of all our traditions, ever reminding us to place principles before personalities.

AA Grapevine

AA Grapevine is AA's international monthly journal, published continuously since its first issue in June 1944. The AA pamphlet on AA Grapevine describes its scope and purpose this way: "As an integral part of Alcoholics Anonymous since 1944, the Grapevine publishes articles that reflect the full diversity of experience and thought found within the A.A. Fellowship, as does La Viña, the bimonthly Spanish-language magazine, first published in 1996. No one viewpoint or philosophy dominates their pages, and in determining content, the editorial staff relies on the principles of the Twelve Traditions."

In addition to magazines, AA Grapevine, Inc. also produces books, eBooks, audiobooks and other items. It also offers a Grapevine Complete subscription, which includes the print magazine as well as complete online access, with new stories weekly, AudioGrapevine (the audio version of the magazine), the vast Grapevine Story Archive and current online issues of Grapevine and La Viña. Separate ePub versions of the magazines are also available. For more information on AA Grapevine, or to subscribe to any of these, please visit the magazine's website at aagrapevine.org or write to:

AA Grapevine, Inc.
475 Riverside Drive
New York, NY 10115

Alcoholics Anonymous

AA's program of recovery is fully set forth in its basic text, *Alcoholics Anonymous* (commonly known as the Big Book), now in its Fourth Edition, as well as in *Twelve Steps and Twelve Traditions*, *Living Sober*, and other books. Information on AA can also be found on AA's website at www.aa.org, or by writing to:

Alcoholics Anonymous
Box 459
Grand Central Station
New York, NY 10163

For local resources, check your local telephone directory under "Alcoholics Anonymous." Four pamphlets, "This is A.A.," "Is A.A. For You?," "44 Questions," and "A Newcomer Asks" are also available from AA.